213/7

FROM
TREE
TO
TABLE

FROM TREE TO TABLE

**GROWING BACKYARD
FRUIT TREES
IN THE PACIFIC
MARITIME CLIMATE**

BARBARA EDWARDS • MARY OLIVELLA

SKIPSTONE

Published by Skipstone, an imprint of The Mountaineers Books
Printed in the United States of America
14 13 12 11   5 4 3 2 1

Copy Editor: Amy Smith Bell
Design: Jane Jeszeck, Jigsaw, www.jigsawseattle.com
Cover Illustration: Lida Enche, www.lidaenche.com
Pruning Illustrations: Ani Rucki
Author photo on page 207: Kyla Collins
Plant Hardiness Zone Map, courtesy of USDA/ARS and adopted by Jennifer Shontz, Red Shoe Design

ISBN (paperback): 978-1-59485-518-4
ISBN (ebook): 978-1-59485-519-1

Library of Congress Cataloging-in-Publication Data
Edwards, Barbara
  From tree to table : growing backyard fruit trees in the Pacific
maritime climate / by Barbara Edwards and Mary Olivella.—1st ed.
      p. cm.
  Includes bibliographical references and index.
  ISBN 978-1-59485-518-4 (pbk.)—ISBN 978-1-59485-519-1 (ebook)
1. Fruit—Northwest, Pacific. 2. Fruit trees—Northwest, Pacific. 3.
Fruit—California. 4. Fruit trees—California. I. Olivella, Mary,
- II. Title. III. Title: Growing backyard fruit trees in the Pacific
maritime climate.
  SB355.E39 2011
  634.09795—dc23
                    2011019168

Skipstone books may be purchased for corporate, educational, or other promotional sales. For special discounts and information, contact our Sales Department at 800-553-4453 or mbooks@mountaineersbooks.org.

Skipstone
1001 SW Klickitat Way, Suite 201
Seattle, Washington 98134
206.223.6303
www.skipstonebooks.org
www.mountaineersbooks.org

 Printed on recycled paper   LIVE LIFE. MAKE RIPPLES.

To Craig, who cheers me on with love and humor,
and to Claire, Eli, and Kyla, who were raised
with the trees. I wish you all just the right balance
of sunshine and rain.

~BARBARA EDWARDS

To my husband, Bill, who teaches me daily about
laughter and love. And to my daughter, Erin—in many ways you
were my inspiration to start this project. For you and all who follow,
may there always be fruit trees.

~MARY OLIVELLA

CONTENTS

If you love me, if you love, love, love me,
Plant a rose for me,
And if you think you'll love me for a long, long, time,
Plant an apple tree.

~FROM THE SONG "IF YOU LOVE ME" BY MALVINA REYNOLDS

Acknowledgments

This book began with conversations with backyard gardeners who offered their fruit tree triumphs and challenges and moved on to questioning and listening to expert horticulturists who generously shared their wisdom, experience, passion, advice, and encouragement. Ann Ralph, whose knowledge of fruit trees is vast and whose enthusiasm is contagious, was an inspiration and soul mate in the developmental stages of the book. Huge amounts of gratitude go to Sam Benowitz of Raintree Nursery, whose experience and expertise were invaluable in helping to explain multiple aspects of growing fruit in the northernmost climes covered in this book. An equal measure of gratitude goes to Jim Gilbert of One Green World, whose knowledge about fruit trees is comprehensive and who couldn't have been more gracious in giving assistance

and answering endless questions. Marc Robbi of Rolling River Organic Nursery shared his wide-ranging experience in planting and caring for fruit trees in many maritime climates. We are grateful to Jake Mikolajcik of Mid City Nursery, Travis Woodard of Urban Tree Farm, Ram Fishman of Greenmantle Nursery, and Paul Doty of Berkeley Horticultural Nursery for their thoughtful consideration in providing information and compiling lists of trees best suited to their respective areas.

An immense thank you to Leslie Miller of Girl Friday Productions, who believed in this project and found a home for the book at Skipstone. Leslie also did an absolutely awesome job of finding and compiling fabulous recipes from fantastic chefs up and down the coast and writing the informative introductions to each recipe. Endless thanks go to those talented and creative chefs who share their genius and give us the keys to turn our fruit harvests into gourmet dishes.

A special thanks goes to Lisa Scott Owen of The Mark Restaurant in Olympia, Washington for her gracious ability to develop the perfect recipes we needed to round out our collection, and to Claire Chessen, who connected us with people who cook some of the best food in San Francisco. We also send special thanks to Karen Belford and Paul Miller, who read and edited early versions of the manuscript, and Jon Polland and Chuck Toombs, who provided invaluable professional advice along the way.

Barbara is forever thankful to her grandparents, whose home was always fragrant with fresh-cut flowers, fruits, herbs, and vegetables, for instilling the love of growing and respect for dirt and the bounty it provides. In writing this book, she is beyond grateful to husband Craig, who steadily encouraged and asked just the right questions. Barbara's children continually inspire and motivate her by sharing their love of wonderful food and their ability to cook it so well. Her family dinner table will be laden with dishes made from the recipes in this book for years to come.

Mary thanks the land itself of Panama, which originally showed her how the magic of life is unstoppable. In developing this book, Mary knows it would not have been possible without her husband Bill's wisdom in helping to navigate the many twists and turns as it evolved. And lastly, Mary has the deepest heartfelt thanks for her daughter, Erin, whose very presence on the planet is a daily source of inspiration and joy.

Introduction:
Plant a Fruit Tree and
Join the Revolution

Don't be afraid to go out on a limb. That's where the fruit is.

~ H. JACKSON BROWN

Sun-warmed fruit eaten straight from the tree is one of life's great simple pleasures. Close your eyes and imagine the sweet smell of pears ripening on the counter, or the aroma of Meyer lemons fresh from your garden. A savory peach and sweet corn salad made with fruit that hung on your tree minutes before slicing will deliver delight magnified by pride in your harvest. Fruit trees bring reverence for the cycle of life and thankfulness for what the earth freely gives. The first time you watch your child wander over to the backyard apple tree, tug off a ripe apple, and climb up onto a low fork in the tree to enjoy it, you'll be so thrilled at how well the small amount of work you did in planting and caring for the tree has paid off that you just might wander out and join her.

Our romance with fruit started with a fig tree and an apple tree. Mary grew a fig tree from a branch she cut from a sprawling and venerable Black Mission fig. The branch has grown into a well-loved and carefully maintained fourteen-foot centerpiece in her front yard that bears armloads of mouth-watering fruit. For more than a generation Barbara's grandmother had an apple tree that supplied two families with enough apples for fresh eating, pies, sauces and salads, as well as jars and jars of spicy apple butter. After moving to the West Coast, Barbara planted her own apple tree—a Cox's Pippin that bears enough fruit to share with her children and their families. Easy access to free and delicious fruit coupled with the pleasures of growing enticed Barbara to plant many more fruit trees over the years in her small plot of land and in the garden of the school where she taught.

When Mary's hopes to reclaim her backyard from under a layer of concrete became a reality, she saw great possibilities for expanding the homegrown fruits in her salad bowl and on her stove and grill. She daydreamed about the pleasures of apricots, persimmons, pears, and more, just feet from her backdoor. To help plan her baby orchard, Mary called on her friend Barbara, whom she knew was an avid fruit grower and loved a good project. The unusual hillside climate of wind, extreme sun, or socked-in coastal fog at Mary's home highlighted the importance of choosing fruits and fruit varieties that could best thrive despite, or maybe because of, these conditions. This led us to both formal (books, websites, and talking to expert nursery professionals) and informal (conversations with neighbors) research.

Along the way we both fell for trees that we just couldn't live without. Mary chose and planted several that are now happily thriving, and Barbara found space to welcome more fledglings into her crowded but fruitful garden. We freely admit to being tree lovers who can't help but spread the word about the pleasures of backyard fruit. Consider this book a conversation you might have over the backyard fence with neighbors who are bursting to share their stories of success. We hope this book will inspire and encourage you to plant fruit trees that are best suited to the climate conditions in your backyard. It's easier than you think.

In addition to being part of our own small stories, planting fruit trees is part of a much larger story about people growing their own food. The movement toward growing and eating local food—food that is grown and consumed within a hundred to two hundred miles—aims to improve the health of our families and the health of our planet by encouraging people to eat food grown nearby instead of from the other side of the world. That Chilean-grown apple that was picked long before it was ripe, now tired after a long sojourn in cold storage, can never compete with the taste and the snap of your own fruit's taut skin. Nor can it compete nutritionally with the vitamin-rich fruit allowed to ripen on the tree. Local fruit is seasonally appropriate fruit. It's often easy to forget that there are seasons for fruits because some semblance of that fruit is always present in the supermarket, usually coming from a different hemisphere. Experiencing the fruit at its best and in its own season usually only happens these days at farmers markets or in the fruits you grow yourself.

Like the movement to eat local food, conversations about the need for future food security are becoming more frequent. Municipalities are encouraging and sponsoring the planting of long-lived fruit and nut trees on public lands and in the community gardens that are sprouting up in vacant spaces in cities large and small. In these days of increasingly expensive and ever-decreasing supplies of fossil fuels, moving food thousands of miles when it can be grown a few miles or even a few feet away is folly. Locally sourced food may give us a reliable supply of healthful calories and contribute to more resilient, self-sustaining communities. Some people go as far as to call the local food movement a revolution. Plant a fruit tree and join! It might be a stretch to think of yourself as a revolutionary as you push your shovel through the soil, making a hole big enough to plant the skinny upright branch that the catalog promised would grow up to bear baskets of pears. But if there is a revolution brewing, putting even one fruit tree in your backyard or on your patio will make you part of it.

If you are looking for great taste and nutrition, secure local food, and an all-around solid long-term investment, you could do no better than to plant a tree with the potential of providing food for you, your children, and possibly your grandchildren. If you plant a long-living fig or pear tree, picture your great-grandchildren thanking you for their breakfast fruit.

This is a love story. By planting a fruit tree, we have beauty and bounty today, and we give a gift to ourselves and to all those who follow.

How to
Use This Book

*First question I ask someone looking for a fruit tree is,
"What do you like to eat?" and the second one is,
"How much space do you have?"*

~ JAKE MIKOLAJCIK, MID CITY NURSERY

Your happiness and success in growing the best-tasting and healthiest fruit just a few steps from your back door are primarily dependent on two things: selecting the right tree and understanding it. This book helps you do both. To understand growing fruit and helping it thrive, we give you information and tips—lots of them—and an overview of tending fruit trees that is applicable to all fruit trees, starting with how to assess the conditions in your yard before you buy your tree, what to look for when choosing a tree, ways to maximize your fruit yields for the amount of growing space you have, and then getting the tree into the ground and the best time to put it there.

To continue to foster the trees you welcome into your care, we offer you the lowdown on food, water, pollination, and methods of providing these essentials for your fruit tree. This chapter is followed by some of the challenges you and your tree may face from other living creatures and how to overcome them as well as possible. Pruning, the process of cutting out branches to achieve and maintain the right size for your trees and to keep your tree producing abundant and tasty fruit, is described in the next chapter. You'll refer to this section repeatedly over the years.

Then we move into our favorite part of the story—closeups on particular fruits. These closeups tell you more about each fruit's specific characteristics, needs, or proclivities, followed by lists of varieties that are most likely to succeed in your specific climate area. Next, each of the main fruit types is featured in recipes to help you use your fruitful bounty in the most delicious ways imaginable. You'll take a gastronomic journey along the Pacific coastal regions, spanning three states and one Canadian province.

In the back of the book we include a substantial glossary of terms as well as a resources section for further guidance. To help you select the right tree, we offer you a range of options that are established by growing conditions in the Pacific coastal maritime climate, the coastal areas between San Francisco and Vancouver, B.C., from the mountain foothills to the Pacific Ocean—all of which share temperate winters and often cool summers. However, within this eight-hundred-mile-long swath of land, there are climate differences that can affect which fruit tree can best be grown. To help simplify some of these differences, we have divided up our fruit tree recommendations based on the United States Department of Agriculture (USDA) Plant Hardiness Zone Map, which is widely used as a guide by farmers and home gardeners alike (see the map on page 18).

Keep in mind that these zones are simply broad generalizations based on average coldest winter temperatures. They don't take into account the many other factors that determine which plants will flourish in a zone, such as summer temperatures and microclimates. Microclimates can make all the difference when planting certain kinds of fruit. A microclimate is the climate of a certain area that is different from the area around it. Microclimates can be very small—the protected spot under an eave in a courtyard, for example—or relatively larger, like a miles-long strip of land next to a large body of water. Cities especially have widely varying microclimates because of human activity, paved areas, and redirection of wind, sun, and shade. There are microclimates even in your own garden that may influence how a variety grows, so careful investigation of your yard is a good idea.

List of Recipes

The coastal region from San Francisco to Vancouver, B.C. is famous for world-renowned chefs and cookbook authors who favor the use of fresh, local produce in their culinary creations. These recipes have been collected from many of those creative chefs. Starting with breakfast and on through to dessert, just reading the recipe titles will make your mouth water. The recipes for the fruits follow each fruit chapter, so when your own trees start producing basketsful, you will know where to look for delicious ways to use the bounty. In the meantime, trying these recipes out on fruit from the store or farmers market is perfectly fine.

Breakfast and Condiments

Salads

Starters

Main Courses

Desserts

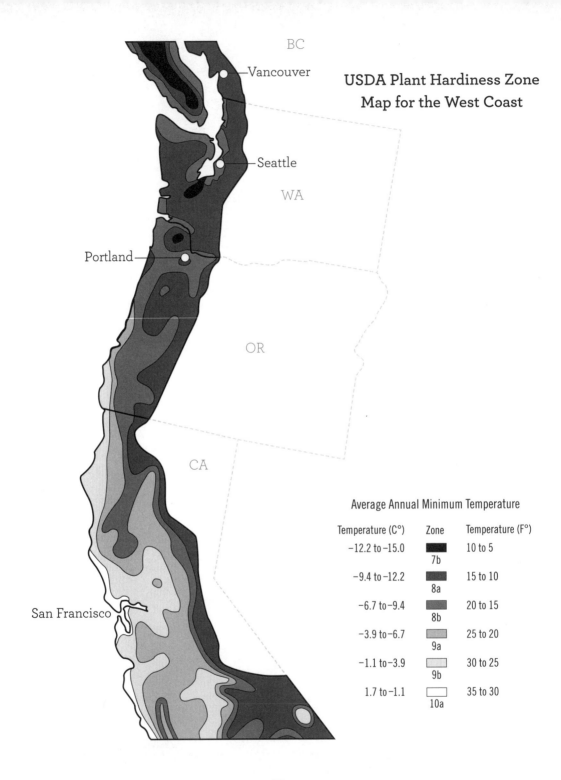

USDA Plant Hardiness Zone
Map for the West Coast

BC

Vancouver

Seattle

WA

Portland

OR

CA

Average Annual Minimum Temperature

Temperature (C°)	Zone	Temperature (F°)
−12.2 to −15.0	7b	10 to 5
−9.4 to −12.2	8a	15 to 10
−6.7 to −9.4	8b	20 to 15
−3.9 to −6.7	9a	25 to 20
−1.1 to −3.9	9b	30 to 25
1.7 to −1.1	10a	35 to 30

San Francisco

Part I
THE FINE ART OF COASTAL FRUIT GROWING

Your garden—a piece of land that can welcome fruit trees that first grew in such far-off lands as Afghanistan, Arabia, China, Eastern Europe, India, the Malay Archipelago, Russia, and Turkey. Human beings have been part of the cycle of seeds and seasons and sustenance for thousands of years. Some of the ancestors of the trees that you can grow in the Pacific coastal regions today were living in the years 5,000 to 11,000 BCE. Food gardening is the oldest type of gardening on Earth. Many of us may remember fruit trees gracing our grandparents' yards. This part of the book provides an overview of how to get started to successfully grow fruit trees at home, even if you have very limited outdoor space. Unfortunately, edible plants are seldom included today in landscaping plans even though foodscaping can be both beautiful and bountiful. You are about to change all that, or at least start the journey with a first step.

1
First Steps

People love to share what they know.
Get the best local advice you can.

—SAM BENOWITZ, RAINTREE NURSERY

There is an old saying that if you want to learn how to garden, heed the advice of experts, but if you really want to learn how to garden, listen to your neighbors. If you really want to know what will grow best at your house, start by studying the kinds of trees you find in your neighbors' yards. Nothing is better than proven success in your particular microclimate. Many of your neighbors have been gardening for years, especially the senior citizen next door or down the street.

Undoubtedly they have observed their trees over the years, possibly decades, and tried various methods to improve their harvests. You could benefit from their knowledge. Take a walk around your neighborhood. Remember to look up as you walk along. In the spring look for the blossoms, and in the summer and fall the fruit will be evident. When you spot that great tree, note its location in relation to the house and other trees as well as its orientation to the sun.

When you see a thriving fruit tree in your neighborhood, check to see if your neighbor is outside so you can casually grill the owner on how she or he helped such a fine specimen to flourish. If you never run into the neighbor, leave a note by his or her front door with a request for information and your phone number. This will often result in a conversation with a person who is bursting to share his or her stories of success or fruit tree woes. Remember to ask about these items:

- What is the specific variety? This is the most important question. "Variety" in this sense refers to trees that are somewhat different from others of the same type.
- How many hours of summer sun does the tree get?
- Do you use a fertilizer? If so, what do you use and how often, and at what time of year?
- What about watering? If you water, how often?
- Do you prune? When? And what do you think about when deciding what to prune?
- Do you thin the fruit?
- Are there any pests or diseases to worry about? If so, what do you do about them?
- How long was it after planting before the tree bore fruit?

FRUIT NETWORKING

Many neighborhoods are connected on an email network. Sending out a request asking for advice on what fruit tree varieties are being grown in your locale could bring up tons of information about trees tucked in backyards that you aren't able to see from the sidewalk. One woman who resignedly thought cherries would never grow in her foggy locale was thrilled when she found out through an offhand comment on the neighborhood email list that a woman down the block had a tree laden with Montmorency cherries. She lost no time arranging a site visit.

Understanding Your Location

What can your backyard offer a new fruit tree? What can the tree offer you beyond its fruit? Where will a fruit tree be happy in your yard? Chilly summers, fog, and cloud-reduced light and winds play havoc with fruit-bearing plants. Many of the trees described in this book enjoy the sunniest part of the yard and standing near the house to benefit from its radiant heat. But other fine specimens are also toughing it out in partial shade or in a location with full wind and fog exposure. Their fruit is reported to be just as plentiful and sweet, so you need not necessarily give up if you do not have an ideal spot for your trees. Perhaps the best site would be a gently sloped area with plenty of sun and radiant heat, with some protection from the wind. But take heart: Trees in many, many gardens without this level of luxury still grow thriving fruit.

Take a walk around your yard to study where your intended trees will be content putting down roots. Which area gets the most sun, preferably a southern or western exposure? For frost-tender trees, is there an area next to a dark-colored, south-facing wall, a brick siding, or a patio or driveway that can reradiate heat at night? Overhangs or awnings can also trap and reradiate heat. A boggy, soggy area is not desirable because standing water can cause root damage. Windy days in the maritime climate are a given, and many trees do just fine, but if you have the option, plant fruit trees in a protected area because strong winds can decrease air temperatures and damage fruit.

In addition to thinking about the tree's needs, think about yours. Many people value the aesthetics of fruit trees when selecting a location. Talk about a showpiece—for visual beauty it's hard to beat the blossoms, fruit, and leaves that sometimes change colors in the fall. In the winter the

HOW IMPORTANT ARE CHILLING HOURS?

Deciduous trees lose their leaves and go dormant in the winter for protection from the cold. The dormancy is triggered by longer nights and dropping temperatures. Chilling hours (or "chilling units" as they are sometimes called) usually refer to the number of hours during the months of November through February that a particular fruit tree variety needs for the temperature to be between 32 and 45 degrees Fahrenheit. How long a particular variety needs to "chill" depends on the climate it has been adapted to. When this particular length of time is over, the tree will start its growth again when the soil temperature stays above 45 degrees for a few days.

Evergreen fruit trees such as citrus don't lose their leaves and don't need any chilling hours. The stone fruits like peach and plum need some chill time, and the pome fruits (apple and pear) need more; some apple varieties need the most chill units. If a tree doesn't get enough chilling time, the leaf growth could be delayed or it could make growth only at the ends of the branches. It also may not bloom or set fruit. Making use of microclimates—such as an area that gets shade in winter or a spot at the bottom of a slope where the cold air settles—could be very useful if you are concerned about getting more chill hours.

If you are wondering about having enough chilling units for a tree variety that you have your heart set on, check with your neighbors or a local nursery, or you can experiment. In a relatively warm, coastal area you can be reassured with the knowledge that trees can often do just fine and bear abundantly with a third fewer chilling hours than they are reported to need. If you live in a low-chill region, you can't go wrong with varieties especially developed to need less chill. There are plenty to choose from. The Anna apple, for example, was bred in Israel and only needs one hundred to two hundred chill hours; the Fuji needs fewer than four hundred, but don't automatically dismiss that Cox's Pippin because you read that it needs eight hundred to one thousand chilling hours. In the San Francisco coastal region, which usually gets under five hundred chilling hours each winter, many gardeners are happily growing Red Delicious apples said to need from nine hundred to fourteen hundred chill hours and many other varieties, including the dependable Cox's Pippin.

tree can provide stunning silhouettes of artful gray branches. You can use a single tree to draw the eye to a special focus spot in the garden, or a collection of trees can create a beautiful pattern. Trees can also muffle the sounds from a busy street or noisy neighbors. In the summer they can create shade for outdoor seating or filter the sun on a south-facing window. And of course you will want to select a location that makes it easy to harvest the fruit.

A Few Words About Rootstocks

This discussion about rootstocks is based on an interview with Sam Benowitz of Raintree Nursery. If you save an apple seed from the best apple you ever ate, plant it, and tend it lovingly, it will still bear fruit that will sadly disappoint you. The only way to get that longed-for taste is to grow a branch from the tree that bore the apple you loved. This is true for most fruits. Fruit tree growers make genetic copies by grafting buds or branches (called scions) of desired trees onto specially selected small young trees (called rootstocks). These rootstocks impart desirable traits to the newly grafted tree, such as small size, winter hardiness, early fruit production, or tolerance for heavy soils.

Usually fruit trees are grown on semi-dwarf or dwarfing rootstocks, but just because you put a tree on a semi-dwarf rootstock doesn't mean you know exactly how tall it will get—rather, the height is relative to how tall that particular tree would be if left to grow on its own roots. For example,

a pear on its own rootstock could grow to forty feet, but if that pear tree is grown on a semi-dwarfing rootstock, it will only grow to about half that size. If it was grown on dwarf rootstock, that same pear tree would grow to a third or so of the size it would have been if left on its own roots. But Sam advises that this is not always a hard-and-fast rule: "If you live in an area with lots of rainfall and good soil, your tree will get taller than that same tree would if it were planted in a drier area."

A tree on the most dwarfing rootstock will only grow from four to nine feet tall and can live its life in a container. These very dwarfed trees, whether in a container or in the ground, will probably need to be staked for their whole lives, as they will have small root systems. Dwarf and semi-dwarf rootstocks are most often used for backyard trees and in commercial orchards. There is not much call for fruit trees on standard-sized rootstock these days unless there are hopes for a swing hanging from a high branch someday. An espaliered tree will need a vigorous rootstock because horizontal branches need more vigor than if they were growing upright. When you plant, make sure the graft union is above the ground. If you plant too deep, it is possible that the tree variety will put out its own roots, which are for a very big tree. In that case you could get a full-size tree instead of letting the dwarf rootstock grow the smaller tree you were expecting.

Some rootstocks will sucker. Don't neglect to cut the suckers off at ground

SIZE MATTERS

The biggest surprise for first-time apple tree growers is how fast a fruit tree can get out of hand. Annual pruning is necessary to keep deciduous fruit trees strong and productive, and this pruning, if properly timed, can also be used to dwarf the size of the tree. Pruning vigorously to keep them under ten feet is recommended. More on that in a minute, but first: What's the problem with letting a backyard fruit tree grow extensively year after year? When you buy a bare-root tree in the winter (usually looking like a three-foot stick), it can appear very unassuming, like a Saint Bernard puppy. You've got to think ahead, though. Do you have enough land for a thirty-foot tree such that the roots won't damage the patio or house foundation? Do you realize that the shade it casts will limit what else you can grow in your garden and reduce your options for lounging out in the sun?

Not many of us have the ladders, equipment, or inclination to prune a thirty-foot tree, so you'll probably need to hire an arborist. With simple tools and not much time, it is easy to prune a fruit tree to stay within eight to ten feet. One of the things that stops people from right-sizing their fruit trees is that they think a small tree will not give them enough fruit. However, that's not quite how it plays out. A seven-foot apple tree can produce seventy to a hundred apples a year. True, a thirty-foot tree does create more fruit, but most people don't have the equipment to harvest the upper two-thirds of the tree and that fruit will fall, making quite a mess. You'll either be spending hours with the rake to clean up, maybe even a scrubber if the patio gets soiled, or paying someone else to do this. If you don't clean up the fallen fruit posthaste, you'll find that wasps, which look like bees to some, absolutely love the split and rotting fruit. They come early and stay late, which can put a dent in any plans to eat, drink, or be merry outside.

It's difficult to organically control for pests or diseases in a tree that's out of your reach. Then there's the issue of raking up the leaves each fall. Think about the number of leaves on an eight-foot tree. Now think of the leaves on a thirty-foot tree and imagine the difference in raking time. Aside from aesthetics, raking up leaves and picking up fallen fruit are critical to stopping this year's insect problems and diseases from going forward into the next year. If you keep your tree small, you will enjoy your tree, not just in the early years but for decades to come. Try this: Stretch your arm up as if you are going to pick a piece of fruit from the highest branch that you can reach. That's the tallest your tree should be, or needs to be. Pruning is the solution and it's not hard. Your tree will be healthier and you will be happier.

This material is based on an interview with Ann Ralph formerly of Berkeley Horticultural Nursery in Berkeley, California.

level or they could become more vigor-ous than the tree. If you don't cut them off early, they can mix with the tree and it can be hard to tell which branches are which until it is time to see or taste the fruit. The fruit grown from the rootstock will rarely be as good. When you buy a fruit tree, it is important that the rootstock on the tree you choose is appropriate for the area where the tree will grow. A local nursery should already have taken care of this issue for you, and a good mail-order company will be aware of needs in your locale.

Size: How Should You Decide

Huge backyard or small, size doesn't need to be the determining factor in growing fruit trees. Many standard (regular) fruit trees can grow to twenty-five to thirty-five feet with a similar spread, although they can be pruned consistently to hold them to ten feet. Alternatively, you can fit three trees with dwarf rootstocks in the same area required by a standard tree. The secret is in the pruning. Variety choice and planting techniques can also play a part in determin-ing how large or small your tree will be. We discuss the possibilities here and provide more specific information on pruning in chapter 3.

Keeping Trees Small(er) and Ways to Save Space

If you only have a small space for that apple or pear tree or mini orchard that you have always wanted, don't dismay. You can have your fruit and eat it too. There are some different ways to go: diligently and somewhat radically prune standard-size trees, buy trees grafted onto dwarfing rootstocks, espalier your trees, plant them diagonally or as a hedge, and keep them as small as possible by planting them in a container. It's also becoming more com-mon to see three or four varieties of the same fruit or different kinds of fruit planted very close together, sometimes in the same hole. We've also seen trees with three to six different varieties grafted onto one tree, often espaliered. Let's talk about a few of these space-saving options.

ESPALIER. A beautiful and classic way to save space is to espalier trees—that is, to prune and train trees to be two-dimensional with all the limbs in one plane and often along a fence or a wall or the side of your house. This technique gives plants sun and air and is a great way to grow fruit in a small space. Espaliered trees will produce fewer but larger fruits. Fruit trees do well trained into formal horizontal, candelabra, U-shaped, or fanlike configurations. Or they can be grown flat against a support but in free-form branching shapes. Apple, pear, and citrus trees are great for espalier-ing because of their flexible branches and branching habits. Most nurseries will offer trees already espaliered into simple hori-zontal shapes with two to three branches on each side. To keep the tree growing in two planes, you will simply prune off all branches that do not lie in those planes.

(For more see "The Espalier Technique" in chapter 3, Pruning Deciduous Fruit Trees.)

MULTIPLE GRAFTS ON ONE TRUNK. If you want more than one variety of the same kind of fruit but haven't the space for multiple trees, consider a three-in-one or a six-in-one. This is a single tree (one trunk and rootstock) that has had various varieties of the fruit grafted onto it. For example, one grafted apple tree can bear three to six different apple varieties, or you could grow a "fruit salad" tree with peach, nectarine, apricot, and plum all on one trunk. The different varieties can be selected to ripen at varying times over the summer and fall, thereby extending the length of the harvest or to provide a small selection of various fruits.

MORE THAN ONE TREE IN ONE HOLE IN THE GROUND. Two, three, or four trees planted in one hole—there are no rules about how many trees you can plant together. This is a great space saver and a terrific way to have varieties that ripen successively—an early ripening variety, a midseason, and a late-maturing variety. Choose varieties that will bloom at the same time and can provide pollen for each other, but whose fruit will mature at different times. Dig one large hole and place the trees about eighteen to twenty-four inches apart, propping or staking to keep them where you want them while you shovel the soil back in. The trees can be planted upright or their trunks angled diagonally away from each other.

As Travis Woodard of the Urban Tree Farm says, "It doesn't matter to the tree. This is your aesthetic decision." After you plant the trees, cut each one to about knee high—to an outward-facing bud. It's best if all of the trees are about the same caliper (the same size around). If one of the trees is smaller or looks weaker, place that one on the south side of the planting so it will get the most sun; this will help it catch up to the others. Use summer pruning to make sure the trees stay balanced and none become big enough to shade or crowd out the others.

Growing in Containers

This discussion is based on an interview with Jim Gilbert of One Green World. A tree in the ground can take advantage of nature's offerings. When you plant a tree in a container, you are the ruler of its universe. You give it soil. You give it water. You arrange its access to light. You give it food. You determine its temperature. You are in charge. Luckily, as long as its basic needs are met, your tree will be happy and bear fruit for you—not as much as if it were planted in the ground, but you will get fruit and beauty and often sweet fragrance as well.

Let's start with the tree. Really, you can grow almost anything in a pot, but a tree with a dwarf rootstock will be an advantage with most fruit trees. Some types of fruit do better in pots than others. Columnar apples, for example, are great for containers because they grow slowly, they are easy to cut back, they don't grow side branches, and they bear well. A peach in a pot is more difficult because it just loves to send out those branches. You have to prune aggressively. The container should be big enough to let the tree grow for a while. If you start with a tree in a one-gallon pot from the nursery, choose a five-gallon container as a minimum (a seven-gallon container would be even better). It is important to fill it with coarse, well-drained potting soil. Adding chunks of bark or rocks will help the water drain. Pumice and perlite can be added too.

Now you have your container, you have your tree, you have your soil. It's time to consider that important-in-so-many-ways factor: location. Choose a sunny deck or patio where your tree will get sun for at least half the day. If you are planting a tree that will have to be moved to a warmer place in the winter, now is the time to plan how you will do that. You will kick yourself for not thinking of it earlier if you end up carrying a heavy pot of dirt up a set of stairs or up a hill. Plant just as you would plant a tree

CONTAINER PLANTING FOR FRUIT TREES

If your only outdoor area consists of a sunny balcony, if you want the option of taking a tree with you if you move, or if you have your heart set on fresh lemons in the winter and you live in a frosty-winter area, container gardening is a viable option. Granted, trees in containers will produce fewer fruit than a larger tree in the ground, but a modest crop may just be enough. Citrus, figs, pomegranates, jujubes, guava, and even cherries will happily grow and produce a small harvest of regular-sized fruit.

To begin, let's talk pots. Consider planting in plastic. If you live in an area where the tree you are growing needs protection inside from cold weather, you'll be relieved in late fall when it's time to move the tree. You can always use a plastic pot placed inside a more stylish pot. Another good idea is to place the container on a plant dolly with wheels if it will be moved on a horizontal surface. Putting screen over the holes in the pot with an inch or more of small gravel on top of the screen will help keep the dirt from washing out.

Before planting, examine the roots of your tree to see if the tree was too crowded in its last container and has become rootbound (the roots spiral around and fill the container, leaving little room for soil and water). If so, the tree will not grow well even in a bigger container. Cut out about a third of the larger roots and gently pull the others apart. Now you can put some soil in the container, position the tree so that the mark where the trunk met the soil in the last container is two or three inches below the rim of the new container, and add the rest of the soil. Tamp the soil gently but firmly around the trunk and water thoroughly. If you want to put a bark or gravel mulch around the tree, now is the time to do it.

in the ground, loosening up the root ball if needed, and water thoroughly. Jim's advice is to "really soak the plant the first time you water and, from then on, be careful not to overwater." He is often surprised that even people who know a lot about plants and growing tend to overwater. Once the plant begins growing, water deeply once a week or twice if it is hot outside. Because it can't draw any resources from the ground, your potted tree depends on you for the food that is critical to its continued health and fruit production. Give it some compost or organic fertilizer each spring.

The matter of temperature depends on the type of tree you are growing and where you live. In general, if the temperature falls below freezing and stays that way longer than overnight, you have to keep the soil from freezing solid and killing the roots. Putting the potted tree in an unheated garage or shed will give it protection from freezing but still allow it to get the chilling hours it needs to give you a harvest. Many fruit trees need between six hundred and a thousand hours of winter temperatures between 32 and 45 degrees Fahrenheit. It might be tempting to bring your little tree into your living room to pamper it gently after a few weeks of cold weather, but hold off. It just might think that spring has arrived and put out buds or bloom way too early.

If you are growing citrus or any subtropical trees and your winters are cold, bring your tree inside as soon as it gets nippy. Such trees don't need a chilling period and would love to overwinter in your sunny kitchen. The citrus will be going through a slow growing time, so they only need to be watered about once a month. Here again, Jim reminds fruit tree gardeners to be careful not to overwater.

After a few winters and springs you may notice the water running right through the soil in your container or roots sneaking out the bottom. If so, the plant is rootbound—the container is too full of roots and it is time to repot. Some people don't wait to see any evidence of a rootbound tree and automatically repot every three years. While the tree is out of the pot, you can cut off about an inch of the roots all around and also prune the tree's canopy to balance out the reduced root structure.

Remember, container environments are less forgiving than growing in the ground, but with a little attention and TLC, you can grow fruit even without a traditional yard. Maybe you have a patio or a balcony or a porch or a flat rooftop where you could grow one small tree or a bantam orchard.

2

Bringing Your Tree Home

The sooner you plant your tree, the sooner you'll get fruit.
Get it in the ground and get it growing.

—JIM GILBERT, ONE GREEN WORLD

After talking and consulting, planning and shopping, you are now almost ready to bring the young tree home. You have studied your property and located the most advantageous sites to start your fruit adventure. You've consulted with neighbors, you've read through our list of tree varieties for your climatic zone (see Part II of this book), and you've talked to the local nursery people. You've decided on the perfect tree. What else do you need to think about?

A few more things, it turns out. First, you'll need to dig the hole for your tree, and you'll be digging approximately the same size hole if you are planting a bare-root tree or one in a pot, so a good shovel will make this job easier. Buying a shovel with a sharp blade and sturdy handle is a very good investment. If you don't want to make that purchase just yet, borrow one from a neighbor or friend or see if there is a tool-lending library in your town, which will let you check out a shovel just as if it were a novel.

Think about how you will get water to your tree. Certainly carrying bucketsful of water to your tree is an option and by next summer could replace a morning at the gym, depending on the distance from the faucet, but it may be easier to use a good-quality hose. As your tree grows larger, a simple soaker hose or high-quality drip system will be more efficient at getting the water to the roots. This will also provide more efficient use of water with less waste.

Timing, or When to Plant

The typical time to buy deciduous fruit trees (such as pears, plums, apples, persimmons, and apricots) is in the winter when they are dormant. This timing is dependent on where you live. If the ground is frozen in the winter in your area, you will be planting early in the spring. If you live where frosty ground is not an issue, you will plant in January or February. Fruit trees are often sold as one-year-old bare-root trees, which means that the soil that they were growing in has been shaken off. Older trees still in pots can sometimes be found at other times of the year, and fall is a good time to plant these, but bare-root trees tend to transplant more successfully. They are also less expensive and easier to carry home. Look for a tree with a straight trunk and well-spaced branches.

The evergreen citrus trees (such as lemons, limes, and mandarin oranges) can be purchased and planted throughout the year, but, if you are planting outside, the best time is in spring after the last frost. If you live in the warmer climates, plant citrus in the late fall to let them take advantage of the winter rains to get established. They are not sold as bare-root plants since they do not have a dormant period.

You'll want to plant your bare-root tree as soon as you can and, if possible, plant on an overcast day. If you can't get it in the ground immediately, keep the tree in the shade and cover the roots lightly with damp soil. If there are a soil ball and burlap around the root, you can wrap the whole ball in plastic until planting.

Planting Your Tree

Think about what your tree's roots will need. The very heavy clay soil often found in the Pacific maritime areas is sometimes problematic because it can become hard like cement, leaving little room for air and inhibiting root growth. This soil doesn't allow good water drainage, and saturated soil roots are susceptible to disease and rotting. Dig a hole twice as wide and twice as deep as the root ball. With a shovel break up the soil on the sides of the hole. Then add back into the hole a small mound of soil (an inverted V). The height of the mound should be such that when you place the root ball on top of it, the tree is at the right level relative to the ground around it. You want the tree to sit at the same level that it did in its previous location. You can locate this point of what was underground and what was above ground by the darkened soil mark on the trunk. If you don't have a helper to hold the tree in the position you want it to grow (usually upright but not always), prop or stake it so it stays the way you want it until the hole is filled with dirt.

One word of caution to the unfortunate few of you who might have moles or gophers in your yards: You'll pull your hair out later if you don't line the hole with wire mesh (easily found in hardware stores).

Refill the hole with the same soil you had removed and tamp it down to eliminate air pockets. Do not mix in fertilizer as this will burn the tender roots. Some trees may appreciate being staked at the time of planting and for the rest of their first year if you live in a windy area. You will especially want to stake young apricot trees as they can easily snap.

Water thoroughly. You can build a watering basin around your tree that extends in a circle slightly past the outer edge of the tree's leaves. Using mulch is a big help in conserving moisture. Mulch also cools the soil in summer and helps prevent weeds. If you use organic mulch (such as compost, bark, wood chips, or straw), your soil will benefit as the mulch decomposes. You can pile that organic mulch up to six inches thick, but don't let it touch the trunk as the constant moisture could invite disease.

You've done it. Now, if you like, you can say a word of welcome, stroke a limb or two, and give a little bow or a nod of the head in a wholesome welcome of this friend into your life.

Food for Thought—and Trees

As Paul Doty of Berkeley Horticultural Nursery says, "It's better to get your tree established in its native soil than to pamper it with amendments. In the long run it has to deal with your soil." Many gardeners report that they have never fertilized their trees and are pleased with their crop yields,

and others fertilize their trees religiously every year in late winter or early spring. One experienced gardener says an occasional watering with compost tea from her worm bins is the secret to her beautiful and abundant fruit.

The experts are in disagreement over how often, or even if, fruit trees need fertilizing. Most often, the experts say fruit trees do just fine with minimal fertilizing as long as the tree is growing well. Your tree might need a little food from time to time, mainly nitrogen, phosphorus, and potassium—all of which can be provided by organic fertilizers. Beware of adding too much nitrogen though, as it can give you vegetation that grows too fast, produces too little fruit, and weakens the tree's resistance to disease and pests. The best time to fertilize is in the spring, and the best food is compost, aged manure, or grass clippings placed around the tree, pushed back about six inches from the trunk. If none

COMPOST TEA

A delight for your fruit tree! Make compost tea by mixing a shovelful of regular compost or a trowelful of vermicompost in a five-gallon bucket of water and let it steep for a day or more—and voilà!—fertilizer. If you use a worm bin for your vermicompost, the brown liquid that drains into the bottom is a top-of-the-line fertilizer when diluted with water.

of those options is available to you, a good all-purpose commercial organic fertilizer is just fine. The other elements that trees need for normal growth are usually available from air and almost all soils.

Make Your Own Compost

Adding compost to soil improves it in every way. It makes heavy soils lighter and able to drain more easily and helps sandy soils retain water. Compost is brown gold for your trees. It isn't difficult to make compost.

If you are in no hurry for the finished product, you can do as many of your great-grandparents may have done in their backyards. Dig a small pit in the ground and throw vegetable kitchen scraps into it and cover them with a shovelful of dirt until the pit is full. A board on top may be necessary so no one steps into the pit. Leave it for the winter, and in the summer you can dig up the rich compost or leave it there to enrich the soil.

If you have quantities of yard trimmings as well as kitchen scraps, fill a commercial or homemade compost bin with alternating layers of chopped-up green and brown vegetative matter and soil. To speed up the decomposition process, turn the pile weekly with a pitchfork into another bin of the same size. To make this turning process much easier, many tumbling or turning composters are comercially available that put out ready-to-use compost without much work. Those old fruit peels, cores, and rinds can help you grow more fruit—and more delicious fruit.

Worm Composting

Arguably, the easiest way to make a fantastic plant food is vermiculture, or worm composting. The little red wriggler worms are the workhorses of decomposition, turning your kitchen scraps into luscious, rich food and compost tea for your plants. Vermicompost is full of nutrients and microbes that help plants use the nutrients that are already in your soil. Kids are often fascinated by worms, and the little red wrigglers, which are smaller and wigglier than earthworms, put on a lively show amid the eggshells when the top covering of shredded newspaper is moved away.

Look for small, oval, amber-colored worm eggs in your bin to reassure yourself that your worms are healthy. Add food scraps at regular intervals, and not too much all at once because the fruit flies will see the riches as their invitation to dine. Commercial worm bins are small, and it's usually not hard to find a place for one close to your kitchen door. Because these bins rarely have an odor, some people keep them in the basement or garage.

If you construct a compost pile on the ground and get busy and forget all about it for several months, you may find that red wigglers have found this ready pile of food on their own and are hard at work breaking it down for your use. When their job is done, they move off to look for better chow somewhere else and you are left with rich crumbly fertilizer.

Watering 101

To harvest big juicy fruits, make sure your tree gets adequate water. If not, your fruit may be smaller than normal as well as less juicy. Your tree may also be more prone to insects and disease. But be careful—don't water too much. Soggy soil can even kill some trees, especially cherries and citrus. A new tree with its short root system will need watering weekly for the first two summers it comes to live with you.

Water deeply enough to saturate the root area. A little water on the surface will not quench your tree's thirst at all. Well-established trees, with their long roots, may need deep but infrequent soakings—one to three times a summer—or even no watering at all, depending on your soil and climate.

To decide how much water your tree needs, you will have to keep a few things in mind. Sandy soils dry out relatively quickly and clay soils retain water. Hot microclimates or long periods of high heat will have you turning on the faucet more often than if the summer is cool or your tree is in a moist area with heavy clay soil.

Water goes straight down and doesn't spread out through the soil unless your tree is planted on a steep slope. When your tree is newly planted, it needs the water to be concentrated just over the root ball and planting area. As time passes, and the roots spread out into the soil, the water application should be moved away from the trunk and be more diffused on the ground just within the drip line (the ground under the outer leaves of the tree) all the way around

GREAT GROWING DEBATES

There is a lot that successful fruit tree growers agree on. In some aspects of growing, everyone agrees: water your bare-root tree well after it is planted, for example. In other aspects, if you talk to ten gardeners, backyard gardeners as well as experienced commercial growers, you might come up with five or six or maybe even ten different ways of dealing with a particular fruit tree issue. One person might tell you to water your apple tree weekly, while another is sure that watering twice in the summer is sufficient, and still another says that an established apple tree never needs watering.

Differences of opinion also come up with fertilizing, pruning, and harvesting. The interesting thing is, they could all be correct! There are so many variables in gardening that there is rarely one perfectly right way to do things. There are fruit tree owners who do almost nothing with their trees or who do everything "the wrong way" and still bring in the biggest harvests on the block. So don't worry too much about getting things exactly right— who really knows exactly what that is?

the tree. This can be easily accomplished with a soaker hose or a drip-irrigation system. Both of these methods will have the added advantage of conserving water.

Pollinating the Blossoms

Every fruit tree originally came from a seed, and like all other organisms it is the goal of every fruit tree to produce more seeds. Luckily for us, those seeds are in the middle of a food we find delicious, and we want our trees to make lots more seeds with food around them. To ensure our fruit crop, we need a little—well, a lot of—help from the pollinators, which are usually insects (but sometimes butterflies and bats and birds). The pollinators visit the fruit tree flowers with their own agenda of gathering food for themselves, but without even knowing—or caring—they are working for the tree and for us.

Fortunately for the tree and for us, one flower provides only a tiny bit of pollen or nectar, and each insect has to visit many flowers to get enough to make a meal or accumulate enough pollen to take back to its hive or nest for storage. While the pollinator is going from one fruit tree blossom to the next, it is mindlessly brushing pollen from the anthers of one flower and letting that pollen fall or be brushed onto the stamens of another flower, either on that same tree or the one next to it or even the one down the block.

If the tree variety you have planted is self-fertile (sometimes referred to as being "self-fruitful"), an insect only has to buzz in and out of the blossoms on that one tree for the flowers to be fertilized and start their journey toward developing seeds. If you have a variety that needs a pollenizer (another tree to provide pollen), the insect must visit blossoms on both trees to transfer pollen back and forth. Nothing is as vital to a successful fruit crop as the pollinators. For that reason we want to invite them into our yards and make their lives as easy as possible.

Busy Bees

There have been a number of alarming reports about the significant decline in honeybees in the United States and the problems this is causing the agricultural industry, so many backyard beekeeping enthusiasts are starting honeybee hives or colonies of native mason bees. You can share the love for these winged creatures that are so necessary to our fruit trees by planting annual and perennial flowers that bloom over long periods in your garden that attract and nourish bees. Several pretty and easily grown options include borage, lemon balm, sweet white clover, lavender, huckleberry, blueberry, fireweed, lamb's ears, lavatera, and sweet alyssum, especially for honeybees and rosemary and lavender for the mason bees.

HONEYBEES (*Apis mellifera*). Backyard beekeepers say that the yields from their gardens and fruit trees make dramatic improvements after the bees arrive. A well-managed hive can produce twenty to thirty pounds of honey annually for your family and lucky friends as well. The rewards of keeping honeybees can be huge, but it is not a project to be taken lightly. It is a commitment and a responsibility as well as a joy.

You don't need much space to keep bees, since they will not stay only in your yard to feed. They travel up to four miles to gather pollen to bring back to the hive. Beekeeping is allowed in most municipalities across the country and in some places encouraged. In fact, it is becoming more common in cities for bees to be kept on the roofs of multi-storied buildings, flying in and out, up and down, all over town. Even in big cities, bees will usually find enough flowers and flowering trees to support the hive.

The biggest problem with the honeybee, despite all the benefits, is of course the sting; the biggest roadblock for potential backyard beekeepers is their neighbors' worries about the stings. The fears are greater than the actual danger, but if you decide to keep bees in a dense neighborhood, think carefully about their location and consider putting the beehives behind a six- to eight-foot fence, so when the creatures make a beeline for their home, they won't fly right past where your neighbors walk.

To protect from stings, the beekeeper wears a big hat with a net when working with the bees and blows smoke in the hive to calm them before checking on the health of the bees inside the hive or when harvesting honey. There are many different strains of honeybees, and surprisingly, some have more docile dispositions than others. Longtime beekeepers say they can tell very quickly when they go to capture a swarm if the bees were part of a calm or a more easily agitated colony. Getting bees from a known and trusted source is the best way to ensure you are getting a gentle strain.

Learning about beekeeping is not difficult, but there are lots of things to find out about to be successful. Beekeeping classes are gaining in popularity, or you can search for an experienced apiarist to help you get started if you decide you have the time and place for bees. The next time you see local honey sold at a farmers market, or harvest your own, you can think of yet another sweet aspect of your fruit tree!

MASON BEES (*Osmia lignaria*). The mason bee is one of thousands of species of native bees in the United States. Mason bees, also called orchard bees, are increasingly being cultivated for pollination duties. In fact, the mason bee is many, many times more efficient at pollinating flowers, especially fruit tree flowers, than is the honeybee. They are excellent pollinators for early spring blossoms because of their tolerance for cold and wet weather. They fly out early in the morning and work till late in the day. If there's any bee that's busy, it's this one!

They stay close to home too. A mason bee does all of her work within five hundred yards of her nest. If there is enough food for her, she will stay within a hundred yards—a real locavore.

These fascinating dark-colored little insects look similar to a fly and carry pollen under their abdomens instead of on their legs like honeybees do. The masons don't live in large buzzing colonies or hives. Each bee lives in its own mud nest but does like to group together with other masons in one area of hollow grasses or holes in trees left by wood-boring insects. Unlike the European bees, all of the mason females can lay eggs instead of just the queen bee, and they do all of their own work, having no worker bees to do it for them. They don't produce beeswax or make honey, so they have little to defend and will not sting unless you squeeze or step on them.

Invite them to take up residence in your yard by providing a home for them. You can buy a mason bee house or easily make one of your own (see sidebar "Building a Bee House"). Since mason bees need mud to build partitions in their nests, leaving a little wet patch in your yard all summer will keep them inclined to stay and lay eggs, and then their offspring will assist you in producing bountiful fruit next spring.

Pests, Disease, and Varmints

A woman walks up to the counter in a large but neighborly nursery with a leaf in a resealable plastic baggie. The leaf is yellow, curled, and rife with brown spots. "What is wrong with my poor tree?" she pleads. The horticulturalist at the counter studies the leaf, consults a book, calls over another person who asks someone else, until no fewer than four people have tried to diagnose the problem, discussing one possibility after another. Finally, one of them asks, "How much of the tree is afflicted with this problem?" The customer answers, "Just this one leaf."

With a hint of a smile, the horticulturalist slides the baggie with the leaf back across the counter to the vigilant woman, praising her for her diligence in inspecting her tree and telling her to be sure and return if more leaves follow the course of the one.

Just as there is a fine line between being an overprotective parent and an attentive one, it's important to inspect and monitor your trees, being aware of possible problems and ready to take action if need be, but

BUILDING A BEE HOUSE

Follow these easy steps and make your own house for your backyard mason bees:

- Cut a four-by-four-inch untreated block of wood to the length you want, usually twelve to eighteen inches.
- On one face drill 5/16-inch holes most of the way through the wood in a pattern of holes ¾ inch apart.
- Make a small roof with a siding shingle, scrap of wood, or post cap.
- Fasten it to a pole or fence post, or hang it in your yard, so that it has a southern or eastern exposure.

not to panic at the first sniffle or one yellow leaf. Nature has many variations, and sometimes the best course of action is to wait a bit and see what happens. For fruit trees some problems never get big enough to worry about, and some problems resolve on their own or with the weather. That being said, we would be remiss if we didn't give you information about some loathsome players in the fruit tree world and ideas about how to deal with them.

While we would like to hope that our tender treelets will be fine out there in the big world by themselves, the rough truth is that we are all part of larger ecosystems and some of the players want what we consider to be our share of the riches. The voracious moths and fly larvae that chew their way into our fruit and the prolific bacteria and fungi that take up residence on our trees' leaves and branches are just trying to survive and multiply the way nature intended. Our aim is to help you protect your trees in ecologically thoughtful ways.

The following suggestions for dealing with pests are poison free to help protect your family and your fruit. Regarding the use of pesticides to control any of these infestations, one wise neighbor told us, "When about to eat an apple, some people are disgusted with nature's worms, but why not with hidden toxic pesticides? That should turn our stomachs even more."

The Pesky Pests

The primary pests to worry about may vary with your location, but the codling moth is a ubiquitous pest in all coastal zones.

CODLING MOTH (*Cydia pomonella*). The saga of the wormy apple starts with the eggs of the codling moth—the nemesis of apple growers. One neighbor swears that if you

CHICKEN SOLDIERS?

Watching hens strutting and scratching around your yard can be amusing, and some gardeners attest that chickens pecking around under their fruit trees have eradicated their "worm" damage. Because codling moths crawl down to the lower part of tree trunks and top layers of soil to look for a place to overwinter, vigilant hens could easily nab them en route or uncover them. The apple maggot, which pupates in the top two or three inches of soil, is very tiny, and some chicken owners question the hens' effectiveness as a control, but sharp-eyed hens might scratch up and gleefully chow down on quite a number. The jury is out on the chicken as hero in the "worm" control front, but chickens give you makings for compost your trees will appreciate. Plus, you'll get eggs unparalleled in taste by any you'll find in the store.

grow more than one apple tree in your yard, the moths will invariably invade the tree with the tastiest fruit. These worms are actually white caterpillars with a brown head. After feasting on apples, they crawl under loose bark on the tree trunk or other protected spots and emerge as moths in April or May. You will rarely see the moths, but they are small and gray with a coppery-colored band at the bottom of their wings. They lay their eggs on leaves and small fruit, and in about ten days the eggs hatch and the tiny caterpillars feed on leaves and the surface of the fruit for a while before

they start to burrow into the center of your apple. After chomping away for about three weeks, they tunnel back out and find a place to spin a cocoon.

Unfortunately, you can get between one and three generations per year of these busy creatures. Organic gardeners have several ways to reduce the worm problem. Prune the tree so that its interior is light and airy, not overly dense with crossed branches. This makes it less attractive for the moth to alight and lay her eggs. Early ripening varieties are less susceptible to codling moths than fruit that ripens later in the season. If you note early on the telltale brown deposits on the maturing apples (the result of the worms burrowing), you can still manage the situation. Remove the visibly infected fruit and thin the rest so that no apples are touching, as the worms can easily migrate across touching apples. Also, to break the cycle, be sure to pick up and discard any wormy apples that fall from the tree. Bury all these apples or put them in a black plastic bag in the sun for a month. Composting may not destroy all the caterpillars.

You can trap the moths with some success if you use one or more of the following methods when the tree starts to bud in the spring. Try commercial pheromone traps, available at many garden centers, which use an attractant scent surrounded by a sticky surface, or make traps yourself (see sidebar "How to Make a Moth Trap").

To trap the larvae, wrap cardboard tightly around the apple tree trunk about

HOW TO MAKE A MOTH TRAP

To make your own pheromone traps, follow these steps:

• In a bucket, mix together 1 cup apple cider vinegar, ½ cup molasses, ⅛ teaspoon ammonia, and 5 cups water.
• Distribute this into two or three plastic jugs with a two-inch hole cut into the upper half of each one.
• Pour a little vegetable oil in each jug, to provide a film on the top to prevent mosquitoes from breeding.
• Hang up to three of these containers in a small tree.
• The codling moths will follow the wonderful aroma and drown before they can lay eggs on your apples.

eighteen inches above the ground with the corrugations in an up-and-down direction in early spring and again in late summer. At the end of June to mid-July remove and destroy the cardboard and the cocoons inside. Wrap with more cardboard and remove and destroy again sometime between November and January.

Releasing *Trichogramma* wasps in early spring can be very helpful over time. These minute insects (four or five could fit on the head of a pin) don't sting humans but parasitize codling moth eggs. Planting alyssum, cosmos, coriander (cilantro), dill, or mustard under your tree will be an invitation to the tiny wasps to take up residence in your garden.

If you have a small tree, or a big tree and a lot of time, you can resort to making a two-inch slit in the bottom of a paper lunch bag, slipping it over an apple and stapling the bag closed around the fruit. This little trick will also help keep birds and squirrels from sampling your fruit and will prevent sunburn too. Take the bag off for the last two weeks before harvest so the color can develop. You can get the same protection with a plastic bag (snip a tiny hole at the bottom for any moisture to drain out) or a micro-perforated polyethylene bag. As much as possible, become friendly with the ants and earwigs and spiders who also will help in your crusade against the moths. And finally, love the woodpeckers and nuthatches and creepers that nab the caterpillars as they squeeze out of your fruit.

Although these various interventions can certainly help, the goal for organic gardeners is reduction not elimination. It is unrealistic to think that you will have not one wormy apple. Most gardeners accept that they will lose a share of the harvest to the worm but are grateful for the abundance that remains. The point is simply not to let the infestation get out of hand.

APPLE MAGGOTS (*Rhagoletis pomonella*). They're called apple maggots, but they are also fond of cherries, apricots, pears, and plums. Just as their name says, they are the larvae of a fly. You will know if you have problems with the apple maggot if you see bumps or lumps on the outside of your apple and brown threadlike tunnels when you cut it open. You may also see a brown

A HOMEMADE APPLE MAGGOT TRAP

Making a trap for apple maggots takes some time. Put a hole in the top of a thin piece of wood, prime it, and then paint it with fluorescent lemon-yellow paint. Place it in a clear plastic envelope and coat both sides with Tangle Trap paste (an adhesive coating found at most hardware and gardening stores) and hang it in your tree. Replace the envelope when it is covered with insects, but be sure to take the trap out of the tree after one month so you don't destroy too many beneficial insects.

mess inside if several larvae attack one poor fruit. But there are steps you can take to protect your crop. Hang commercially available sticky traps shaped like red balls in your tree. You can also make your own trap (see sidebar "A Homemade Apple Maggot Trap").

Hang the trap (commercial or homemade) in the outer third of the tree by early July. Be sure to pick up and destroy any dropped fruit, because the maggot falls with the fruit and then burrows into the soil. Soak any affected fruit in water for several days, bury it at least one foot deep, or tie it up in a black plastic bag and leave it to cook in the sun for several days. A more labor-intensive, but definitely extremely effective, method is to enclose your fruit with paper or plastic bags or nylon footies (as described in the codling moth section and below).

More and more gardeners have been

PREVENT FRUIT DAMAGE WITH NYLON FOOTIES

Nylon footies (yes, the same little disposable nylon stockings shoe stores give to people when trying on shoes) are proving to be extremely effective in preventing fruit damage from apple maggots. This use was "discovered" by a member of Oregon's Home Orchard Society as he watched his girlfriend slip her feet into some nylon footies. He started experimenting with them on his growing fruit and had good results. Put footies on your apples when they are about nickel sized and after you have thinned the fruit so they don't touch. Bunch up the footie in your fingers like you would if you were putting a sock on a baby, pull the footie all the way up, and twist slightly or pinch it around the stem. The footie stretches as the apple grows. The footies confuse apple maggots because they don't visually recognize the brownish wrapped apple as fruit.

After harvesting, you can collect the footies and wash them in plain water or use a little mild soap. Some will not shrink enough to be reusable but most will. Although there were great hopes for the footie method to vanquish codling moth damage and first reports were very encouraging, gardeners are finding that the footie by itself is not enough to keep that persistent caterpillar away. Ted Swenson of the Home Orchard Society came up with the idea of soaking disposable nylon footies or foot socks in Surround, a nontoxic, finely ground kaolin clay. The nylon footies set up the physical barrier and the clay provides an irritant that keeps the codling moth caterpillars from feeding on the apples. If you use this method, remember to wash your fruit especially around the stem before eating. The substance should come off easily, but if not, use a soft brush to remove any lingering clay.

slipping nylon footies (also called maggot barriers) over their small fruit to keep the apple maggots away (see sidebar "Prevent Fruit Damage with Nylon Footies"). These stretch with the growing fruit and can be washed and reused the next year. Unfortunately, the little flies don't seem to mind the cool coastal climate, although they are a bigger problem in early maturing varieties, so you could try thwarting them somewhat by growing late-maturing varieties, such as the Imperial, Winesap, or Jonathan apple.

SPOTTED WING DROSOPHILA FLY *(Drosophilia suzukii)*. There's a new pest in town. A few years ago the spotted wing drosophila fly moved across the Pacific to take up residence in California. Its offspring—and they are a prolific bunch—have been steadily moving north up the coast ever since. They are fond of fruit on the tree as well as on the ground, and they are partial to cherries but occasionally go after peaches, nectarines, and plums. The spotted wing drosophila is in the same family as the common fruit

MANAGING THE SPOTTED WING DROSOPHILA

The University of California's Integrated Pest Management Program explains the method for control of this pest that has been used in Japan:

- Collect three to five quart-sized plastic yogurt or deli containers with lids.
- With a large nail, punch seven to sixteen holes that are 3/16 inch in diameter around the top halves of each container.
- Insert wires through two holes on opposite sides to hang the traps.
- To first see if the spotted wing drosophila is a problem in your area, bait each trap with an inch or two of white wine, put on the lids, and hang them in your tree three to five feet from the ground. Check these bait traps at least weekly for two- to three-millimeter-long flies with dark spots at the tips of their wings floating in the wine. These are the males, and if you find them, you will know you have the pest.
- Now mix up a solution of ¼ cup grape wine, ¼ cup water, and ¾ teaspoon molasses for each container and put the lids on. (A simpler mixture of one inch of apple cider vinegar and two drops unscented dish soap also works.)
- Hang the traps in shady spots on the lower branches of the tree, changing the bait every few days until harvest is done.
- Don't pour the bait on the ground, though, as it will still smell great to a drosophila fly. If you find just the common fruit fly without the spots in your bait traps, you can relax, although you will want to keep checking, as the spotted wing drosophila has the potential to have up to ten generations of offspring each year!

fly (also known as the vinegar fly), which is attracted to decaying fruit, but this new spotted villainess can penetrate *fresh* fruit skin and lay her eggs just under the skin of your cherry.

When they hatch, the larvae feast on your fruit till they are ready to pupate. The area where the fly penetrates the fruit will turn brown, but an infestation is often not noticed on a backyard tree until harvest. If you notice a "sting" or dimple-shaped spot on that beautiful ripe cherry, it might be for the best to harvest your whole crop. Sort out the cherries that are infested and bury them deeply in the ground or tie them very tightly in a black plastic bag and leave them in the hot sun for several days. Home-composting them is not a good idea because your compost probably doesn't get hot enough to dependably destroy them. We hope that some beneficial creature will discover and start feeding on the spotted wing drosophila in the next few years, but until then traps may help you manage this fly population. Try the method that the University of California Integrated Pest Management Program reports was used in Japan (see sidebar "Managing the Spotted Wing Drosophila").

PEAR SLUG (*Caliroa cerasi*). A pear slug is really a sawfly is really a wasp, but whatever you call it, it is a pest in the northern coastal regions. The larvae eat the leaves on pear, cherry, and plum trees. It looks like a shiny black slug, and when it molts, it turns olive green but it is still just as unattractive to a pear tree owner. The slug munches on leaves, leaving them looking battered with brown spots and holes. Handpicking is effective but not much fun. Wash the slugs off the leaves with a strong stream of water, but choose a sunny day for this because it might take a while.

The Daunting Diseases
PEACH LEAF CURL (*Taphrina deformans*). If your tree is unlucky enough to be affected by the peach leaf curl fungus, you'll see leaves crinkle and curl up. The first sign may be reddish areas on leaves about two weeks after they come out early in the spring. These areas get thickened and puckered, and the leaves start to distort and curl inward or downward, and then they turn powdery and grayish-white and finally brown. At this point the leaves could either stay on the tree or fall. Blossoms and young fruit may also be affected and usually just give up and drop from the tree. Leaf curl mostly affects new growth early in the season, especially in a wet, cool spring. Older branches and leaves and fruit are more resistant to the disease. Later, a second set of leaves is bravely produced by the tree, and these will go on to grow more normally unless the wet weather continues, but sadly fruit production could be seriously affected.

The peach leaf curl fungus is an opportunistic disease. Spores can lodge in crevices in the bark and remain inactive for years if the weather is dry every spring, but if some spring brings frequent rain, the spores germinate wildly and attack new growth.

This periodic infection makes it confusing to home gardeners trying to figure out if the methods they used the year before to control the leaf curl were successful in eradicating it or not.

There are several organic methods of dealing with leaf curl. One widely accepted method is to pick off and remove any affected leaves, including any that drop from the tree. Some gardeners claim that spraying leaves with aerated compost tea (see sidebar "Compost Tea" on page 33) is effective. Even though some gardeners have resorted to using a lime–sulfur spray in the early fall, others have reported that their success with this organically accepted spray was no better than the "removing leaves" method. To have the most success in dealing with peach leaf curl, you must control the weather. Lacking that power, the next best hope is to choose curl-resistant varieties.

POWDERY MILDEW. Powdery mildew on fruit trees can be caused by several fungi that all produce similar symptoms on fruit trees. If you notice a white to gray powdery growth on the leaves that looks like they have been dusted with flour, your tree has powdery mildew. It will cause new growth to be distorted and fruit can develop web-like russeting on the skin.

Powdery mildew fungi travel by wind and develop best with moderate temperatures, high humidity, and shade. If there are only a few affected leaves or shoots on your tree, prune these off and bury them deeply or remove them from your yard. Be sure to disinfect your pruners with a weak bleach solution between cuts. If you have had powdery mildew on your tree in past years, it may be best to take preventative measures. Spray a plant-based oil such as neem or jojoba every two weeks, starting when a bit of green appears at the tips of buds, and continue until tiny fruit has developed. You can also try spraying with a solution of one teaspoon of baking soda, two teaspoons of vegetable oil, and a drop of liquid dishwashing soap to one quart of water. Weekly spraying of a solution of three parts skim milk to nine parts of water is another recommended way to prevent powdery mildew fungus on your trees. Be sure to spray both sides of the leaves.

MICROPERFORATED POLYETHYLENE BAGS

Commercial and home fruit tree growers are experimenting with using microperforated polyethylene bags to protect fruit from damage from, well, everything except the neighbor's kids. Bagging fruit will keep insects and birds off your fruit and allow light to pass through. It is possible to reuse the bags from year to year, cutting down on a little expense, but, more important, reusing them adds less plastic to the waste stream.

APPLE SCAB FUNGUS (*Venturia inaequalis*). This can be the most serious apple disease in coastal areas. Moist, warm spring weather can foster the growth of the wind-borne fungus. In the spring, small pale spots occur on new leaves. The spots enlarge and darken, and the leaves can curl and distort and drop from the tree. Raised brown or black spots appear on the apples and may become corky as the fruit grows. If the infestation is mild, the apples will get a small spot or two but still be fine to eat. If the infestation is severe, the spots will be large and the fruit may become misshapen and drop prematurely.

Prune to promote air circulation in your tree and avoid wetting the leaves while irrigating. The fungus overwinters in the dropped leaves under the tree, so if you rake up and remove the leaves in the fall, the damage from the fungus may be very limited. (Alternatively, don't rake up the leaves but add nitrogen to the leaf litter under the tree to make the leaves decompose more quickly. The earthworms will love you.) Hope for dry weather. If spring weather is dry from the time the leaves start to emerge until fruit has set, the apple scab fungus will not gain a foothold on your tree.

FIRE BLIGHT (*Erwinia amylovora bacteria*). A tree branch affected by fire blight looks, not surprisingly, as if it has been scorched by fire. Fire blight is a homegrown bacterium, originating in the United States and spread to other parts of the world. Fire blight can be

PREVENTING FIRE BLIGHT

The most effective weapon in the fire blight fight is prevention. Try these tips:

- Don't feed your trees too much nitrogen fertilizer, so they don't grow excessive shoots and suckers, which are more susceptible to fire blight.
- Water the ground and not the leaves of your trees.
- Try to catch the problem early by checking your trees often, especially during a wet spring, to notice the first signs of distress.
- Prune off and remove from the area all the branches that are affected, by cutting at least twelve to fifteen inches past the discoloration in the spring and at least four to six inches in the fall or winter.
- It's a hassle but don't forget to clean your pruning tools with a 10 percent bleach solution between cuts. It's sad to have to cut branches, especially those with blossoms—your future fruit—but if you do, your tree will live to bloom and fruit again.
- Your biggest ally in avoiding fire blight is to plant resistant varieties whenever possible.

a problem for pears as well as apples. The list of ways your tree can be infected seems endless and extremely difficult for a grower to have any control over.

If you see any part of your tree, including blossoms, rather suddenly turn dark and watery-looking and quickly wilt and die, you probably have fire blight. Some years you won't see a bit of it, and other years could have all the right (or wrong) weather conditions to enable this bacteria to colonize your tree—mainly warm, wet weather during bloom time. Your most effective weapon in the fire blight fight is prevention (see sidebar "Preventing Fire Blight").

ANTHRACNOSE FUNGUS OR BULL'S-EYE ROT. Bull's-eye rot is such a colorful and unfortunately descriptive name for the anthracnose fungus, which can be a huge problem in the high rainfall areas west of the Cascades and in British Columbia. It causes dead sections of bark, called cankers, on branches and sometimes the trunk of an apple tree as well as pear, quince, and crabapple trees. Spores of the anthracnose fungus usually get on your tree during fall rains but also in winter and early spring. The spores infect twigs and branches through the bark. Cankers appear first as small, round, reddish-brown spots that grow quickly along the branch.

A crack forms inside the boundaries of the elongated spot, and then the infection goes down through the bark. The cankers don't grow much in the winter but can grow quickly in the spring. Usually they form on thin branches less than two inches around, but they can also form on larger branches or the trunk. By late June they have grown as much as they are going to grow, and a crack forms around the elongated canker.

Most cankers are about two to five

CONTROLLING BULL'S-EYE ROT

To control anthracnose fungus, check your branches often in the fall and early winter while it is relatively dry before the fall rains begin. Cut off any small branches if you notice a canker starting; cut the branch several inches below the canker. If you find cankers on large branches or on the trunk, you can try to cut them out with a sharp knife. Make sure to cut the bark along the edge of the canker. Get the prunings out of your yard promptly and also remove any old fruit hanging on the tree.

There are claims that applying 70 percent neem oil, or mixing 1 tablespoon baking soda with 2½ tablespoons vegetable oil in a quart of water, shaking, and then adding ½ teaspoon pure castile soap or dishwashing soap and spraying this on the cankers every week, may also be of benefit to prevent the spores from germinating.

inches long. There may be many on a branch, and if they surround (girdle) the branch, it could die because no water or nutrients are able to go through. As the summer continues, a callous forms around the edge of the canker and some of the dead bark in the canker falls out, leaving, by fall, shredded bark that is suggestive of guitar or fiddle strings on smaller branches. In the fall a year from the original infection, the fungus in the canker forms spores that can cause new infections. The canker won't get any bigger, but it can continue to produce spores for several years with the potential of infecting new areas of your tree.

If you eat your apples within a few weeks of picking, even if your tree has anthracnose fungus, you probably won't notice any problem at all. These apples are fine to eat, but if your apples spend a long time in storage, you may notice slowly developing, distinctive bull's-eye-patterned rotten spots on the skin that are brown on the outside with a paler—sometimes pinkish—center where the spores are growing.

Varmints Competing for Your Fruit

There are bigger creatures with designs on your harvest. First there are the two-legged varmints and those would be the birds, which like to lightly sample or devilishly devour your long-awaited goods. You may be wondering when your peach or cherry fruit is perfectly ripe, but the birds have no such confusion. Somehow they always know to plunge beak into fruit at the precise moment it reaches its optimum

flavor. With a large fruit, you may be able to overlook the birds' transgressions, cut out the poked section, and eat the rest, but with a small fruit like a cherry, the bird wins with just one peck.

As you can imagine, people have spent a lot of time and effort in trying to outsmart the birds with scarecrows, Mylar streamers, clanging lightweight pie pans, bells, plastic hawks or owls, and loud noises and alarms, but the best solution is ¼- to ⅝-inch plastic netting. For a small tree, building a frame to put the netting over will save the fruit on the periphery of the tree as well as the inside fruit, but a frame might be difficult for a larger tree. Simply draping netting over the tree will protect most of the fruit.

The four-leggers come next, and fruit growers all agree that you have to protect your trees from deer that blissfully roam the streets even in many urban areas. The deer can demolish your trees in a single night. Some people are engaged in a constant war, but the only true prevention is to build an eight-foot fence around your yard or tree. The fence does not have to be an imposing eyesore or wall. See-through lattices for the top or a six-foot fence with a bar raised higher at eight feet provides a visually pleasing sense of open space between the wood. A common antideer approach is to encircle the trees with wire cages, but these can be toppled over. Some dog owners swear that their canines can keep the deer away if kept outside at night, but beware of that one night you succumb to that doleful begging to sleep indoors.

Do not be lulled into thinking that deer-repelling products sold in the stores will really keep the deer away. Usually they just smell bad and they discolor the leaves, and are not recommended for use two weeks before harvest time—which defeats the purpose. If deer wander your streets, build the fence or risk heartbreak.

Young trees and dwarf varieties are more susceptible to deer destruction. When a standard-sized or even semi-dwarf tree is fully grown, the deer can't reach high enough to munch on a significant amount of leaves or fruit. You could consider a fig tree, which the deer don't seem to fancy. Also, lemon trees (once mature) can still be prolific and beautiful despite deer nibbling at them occasionally. Then again, there is the Zen approach noted by one soul: "Leave some of your fruit on the ground or outside the fence as an offering for the deer. Don't get resentful when they take their share—they are part of the landscape too."

Raccoons don't cause too much fruit loss in urban areas because there are other, more easily obtained food sources, such as the cat food sitting out on the neighbor's back porch. If you notice big bites taken out of your fruit, however, you may want to wrap your tree trunks up to three feet with galvanized or aluminum circular tubes, such as vent piping or aluminum sheeting. If raccoons are jumping onto your fruit trees from another tree, cut them, if possible, till they are far enough apart to thwart the scoundrels. Skunks would rather you left fruit on the ground for them to eat, but they will sometimes try to climb up and partake of what's in the tree unless you wrap the trunks with metal.

In many yards the most frustratingly damaging creature is the squirrel, who starts, long before your fruit is ripe, to nibble a couple of bites from a few pieces of fruit every day and then chucks each one to the ground, chattering loudly the whole time as if a restaurant had just served it an undercooked meal. On a standard tall fruit tree, wrapping the tree trunk with a two-foot band of metal, six feet off the ground, is a good deterrent to the squirrels because they are nimble jumpers. However, if you have followed all the advice in this book, you won't have a single six- to eight-foot tall trunk, so your best other option is to net your tree with ¼- to ⅝-inch nylon mesh the minute you see that first flick of a bushy tail.

Beneficial Bugs and Plants: The Good Guys

A bug is a bug is a bug, or is it? From a fruit gardener's perspective, there are good bugs and there are bad bugs. The good, or beneficial, bugs pollinate our trees' blossoms to increase crop yields and help get rid of the bad bugs by eating them or by parasitizing their eggs with eggs of their own. Beneficial insects will work for us for food and some leaves to hide under. Who are these good guys? Ladybugs, also known as lady beetles, are beneficial for fruit trees, as are green lacewings and parasitic wasps—the minuscule, harmless-to-humans kind of wasps.

Attracting the good bugs is as easy as attracting the bad bugs. The good little predators eat pollen and nectar as well as other insects. Planting a variety of flowers to ensure blooming throughout the season attracts the good bugs to your garden and encourages them to stay. Grow some cosmos, buckwheat, hairy vetch, mustard, coriander (cilantro), clover, parsnip, calendula, marigolds, alyssum, or dill and provide a sprinkling of water and some leafy plants to protect the good guys from the sun and predation by birds.

Planting lavender and garlic under fruit trees is said to be offensive enough to codling moths to repel them, and it couldn't hurt to try it since both plants are attractive and the combined smell of lavender and garlic is usually pleasing to humans.

Low-growing broadleaf plants such as violets and common yarrow help keep the spores of some of the fungi that affect fruit trees harmlessly down on the ground instead of splashed up into the tree by rain or irrigation.

A delightful benefit of growing the plants on the beneficial list is that when they go to seed, songbirds will come to sing for you as they bustle around the plants eating seeds and insects alike. True, they may eat some good bugs along with the bad, but we can always hope that they like the bad ones best. Watching a small flock of goldfinches excitedly descending on gone-to-seed cosmos flowers and feasting noisily while hanging upside down is completely charming. The following birds feed on both insects and seeds: bluebirds, finches, goldfinches, sparrows, juncos, meadowlarks, orioles, titmice, and towhees. All they need from you is a place to take cover if danger is near.

WASHING YOUR FRUIT

Many of us are happy to transfer a fruit off the tree directly into our mouths, but sometimes it needs a little cleaning first. This is true especially for the low-hanging fruit. Washing with running water is just fine, but another effective and quick cleaning method is to put three parts water to one part vinegar in a spray bottle, spritz it onto the fruit, rub it with your hands, rinse, and eat.

The Big Picture

In the fruit tree realm, we have the allies, the nuisances, and the enemies. The allies (good bugs and good birds) help you get the beautiful fruit you want, the pests (the bad bugs and varmints) just want to share your crop to a greater or lesser degree, and the enemies (the bacteria and fungi) have the potential to destroy the very tree that sustained them. Some of the nuisances can leave you without a crop; others will attack only a fraction of your harvest. You can decide how far you want to go to get rid of the nuisances. Some people, for example, think nothing about cutting out damage caused by the codling moth on their apples, while others would consider an apple with a wormhole inedible.

It's the enemies that you have to be vigilant about. Keeping your trees healthy is the first step in vigilance. Though good health is not always enough protection to withstand all outside assaults, like people, healthy trees are better equipped to withstand pests and disease. Remember to prune for maximum light and ventilation, inspect your trees periodically, pick up all dropped and rotting fruit, rake leaves, encourage beneficial insects, and (maybe the best advice) choose varieties that are resistant to the diseases common in your area.

3

Pruning Deciduous Fruit Trees

Learning to grow things is a process.
You can learn from your mistakes.

—SAM BENOWITZ, RAINTREE NURSERY

There are many opinions about pruning fruit trees. Some opinions call for a relationship with a tree, responding to its individual vigor and growth; other opinions call for managing all fruit trees in the same manner and cutting to a formula. Some pruning tactics were developed in large commercial nurseries, others in small gardens and backyards. Pruning decisions can be confusing but don't have to be intimidating if you follow a few basic guidelines and remember this: Unless you are pruning with a chain saw, your tree will be fine.

For more specific pruning information, be sure to refer to each fruit tree chapter in Part II of this book.

Why prune? The simple truth is, you don't have to prune. Your tree will grow along and even give you fruit for some years, but if you want the most and the best quality fruit and beauty out of your fruit tree for the most years, prune.

Pruning lets the sun shine through the branches to the fruit. Pruning lets you be in charge of the shape in which your tree grows. Pruning gives the tree a strong structure to support the fruit it bears. Pruning keeps the fruit within your reach. That old saying about the best fruit being at the top of the tree refers to an unpruned tree. If you prune, the best fruit will be everywhere.

Pruning Terms

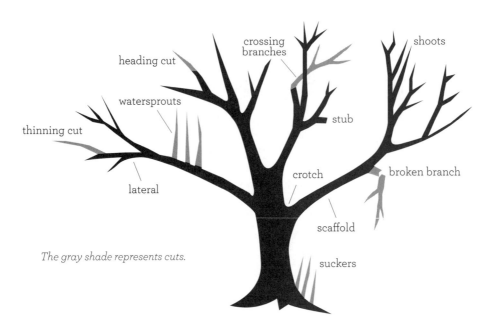

crossing branches

heading cut

shoots

watersprouts

thinning cut

stub

lateral

crotch

broken branch

scaffold

The gray shade represents cuts.

suckers

Cutting Basics

You'll need a few tools. A hand pruner is a necessity, and the bypass type with two sharp blades is most recommended because it makes clean cuts so bark is not damaged. Lopping shears are used for branches thicker than a finger, and a folding handsaw for larger limbs would be nice too. If you plan to let your tree grow taller than you can reach, a pole pruner comes in handy and eliminates the need to climb ladders. Consider the comfort of a pair of good gardening gloves.

There are two kinds of pruning cuts: thinning cuts and heading cuts.

• A **thinning** cut removes an entire branch and is done to reduce the number of branches rather than to encourage the tree to grow more branches. Most of your cuts, especially as your tree matures, will be thinning cuts. A thinning cut should be made at the base of the branch to avoid leaving a stub, but not so close as to damage the thickened area known as the collar, where the branch meets the trunk or a larger branch.

• A **heading** cut removes part of the branch. Side branches will grow from below the site of the heading cut. When heading a branch, cut to a bud (the small beginning stage of a shoot). A bud points in the direction that a new branch will usually grow. If the bud is at the bottom, the new branch will usually grow in a horizontal direction. Because the most vitality on a branch goes to the terminal (end) bud, when you head back a branch, the new terminal bud will now get the most vitality.

People have been pruning fruit trees for hundreds of years, and methods to train trees abound. Fruit trees are often trained into two or three main shapes depending on the style in which a tree naturally grows, and these are described in the pages ahead. These shapes are widely used in orchards to get the best yields and for ease of harvesting. You may envision a completely different shape for your tree based on your aesthetics and your space. Think about how much room you have and how big you want your tree to be, and keep that in mind as you prune. If the space you have for your tree is long and narrow, it is fine to prune your tree to be long and narrow by cutting out those branches that don't fit.

In growing backyard fruit, pruning to keep trees small is usually desirable, but sometimes people eschew all advice about keeping their trees small because they don't want to fence their yards against roaming deer and don't mind climbing ladders or want a large shading tree like one they grew up with. It's your tree and you can do what you want, but it is best to start with a vision. Unless your vision includes a tall tree, right after planting your bareroot tree (if it wasn't already done at the nursery) cut it down to eighteen to twenty-four inches from the ground—roughly even with your knee—and cut any side shoots back to one bud. These may seem like the cruelest cuts, but there is good reason to cut so drastically. Trees grow with a balance of roots underground to branch structure above ground. When the tree was taken out of the dirt where it was growing for its first year, most of its roots were severed, leaving more top growth than roots. Cutting off a portion of the top growth equalizes the top with the root system. Also, cutting to a short stature also encourages the low branches that will give you a head start on maintaining a manageably sized tree.

Tree Shapes

The tree shapes in which trees are most often trained in orchards are the open center shape (most often used for the stone fruits) and the central leader shape (most often used for the pome fruits). In backyards there could be many, many shapes for a fruit tree, including all of the space-saving shapes discussed earlier in this book. It is also becoming more common to train backyard fruit trees in bushlike form to keep them under eight feet tall, as described by the University of California's *The Home Orchard: Growing Your Own Deciduous Fruit and Nut Trees*.

BUSHLIKE SHAPE. This basic cutting method aims to keep a tree small as well as productive, and the instructions are simple. During the first May after you planted your bare-root tree and the new growth is about two feet long, head back the new growth by half. What is left will continue to grow and new shoots will form. In early summer the new growth will be about two feet long—head that new growth back by half. The branches and shoots will keep growing and may need to be headed back again in late summer and possibly again in early fall. When you're heading back branches, you'll need to thin out some of the numerous shoots too, so the sun can shine through to the lower branches and air can circulate. You will want to especially thin out vertical growth and leave more horizontal branches, which will produce the most fruit. In the winter, when it is easier to see the tree's structure, thin out branches that are crowding or rubbing other branches.

Begin pruning in this same way the following spring and summer until the tree reaches the height you want it to be. Now your job is only to maintain the tree at this height and keep it fruitful by continuing to prune during the year in the way just described. In subsequent years cut any growth above the chosen maximum height, and thin crowded branches, especially verticals, and remove any branches that are not fruiting. The easiest way to know which branches are not fruiting is for one of the pruning times to occur during blooming when the leaves are not obscuring the branches.

OPEN CENTER OR VASE SHAPE. This common method removes the central trunk, called the leader, and leaves an open center. It has three to five major branches, called scaffolding branches, that come out from the trunk. The open center shape is best for the stone fruits—plum, peach, apricot, cherry, and Asian pears—whose natural growth habit is more like a vase, but it can be used for all fruit trees. After you have planted your tree and headed it back knee high and

Bushlike Pruning Method

At planting   Spring

Summer

To Maintain Tree Size

removed the side branches, let the tree grow till summer and it has new growth. When the new branches are about four inches long, select three to five little branches that will become the scaffolding branches as your tree grows. Try to choose some that are spaced around the tree and not directly above or across from another one. If they are not already growing out at a forty-five to sixty-degree angle, use the clothespin trick to train them (see the "Training Your Young Tree" sidebar in this chapter). Remove any other growth.

In the second year you will have your original three to five scaffolding limbs and other branches will be growing out from these scaffolding limbs. Select one or two branches on each scaffolding limb. Head these branches to twenty-four to thirty inches and cut off the rest of the branches. To help strengthen the scaffold branches, each year in winter or summer for the first three years, head back the scaffold branches to an outward-growing shoot that is growing in the same direction. As the tree matures, keep the center open by thinning out all vigorous upright growth and water-sprouts (suckers) that grow straight up from the main limbs and also thin branches along the scaffolding branches to ensure light can get to the interior. This thinning pruning can be done in summer or winter.

CENTRAL LEADER SHAPE. This cut is a great choice to let sunlight into the interior of the tree. The central leader shape makes a much smaller tree than the vase shape, and it's good for trees with a naturally upright growth habit, like pear, apple, and sometimes cherry and some kinds of plum. The shape of this tree is like a Christmas tree, big on the bottom and smaller as it rises. It has one main upright trunk—the leader. The first summer after you planted and headed back your tree to knee high, it will have numerous new shoots around the trunk and

Open Center or Vase Shape Pruning Method

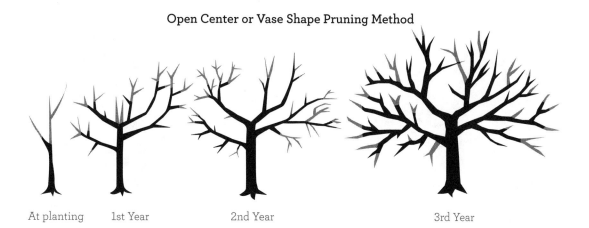

At planting   1st Year   2nd Year   3rd Year

at the top. Choose one upright shoot near the top to become the leader and cut off other vertical shoots that grow within four inches of the new leader. Now your central leader is established and you can choose three to five scaffolding branches starting at twelve to fifteen inches from the ground and evenly spaced around the tree. The branches do not need to be the same distance from the ground but should be spaced in a sort of whorl around the tree. Remove the other branches. Train the small scaffolding branches to have a sixty-degree crotch angle (see the "Training Your Young Tree" sidebar in this chapter).

During next year's pruning, develop a series of scaffolds every two or three feet vertically up the central leader. Some of the branches will not grow out laterally from the central leader and may have to be trained. Once the tree is at the maximum height you want it, prune the leader off to a lower, weaker leader. In the years thereafter cut back the high primary branches to keep the tree's cone shape. Lateral branches without side branches should be headed back by one-fourth of their length to strengthen the lateral branch and to encourage side branches. Head them back to a side shoot close to the same diameter as the lateral being cut. Upright growth and growth with narrow crotch angles can be pruned off in summer or in winter. Summer pruning is the best time to remove unwanted side shoots and excessive growth. After your tree is two or three years old and your basic shape is established, shift to pruning to maintain the shape and height and allow sun and air to reach the interior of the tree.

The Best Time to Prune

Winter? Summer? Spring? Here's where experts often disagree. Some say do your

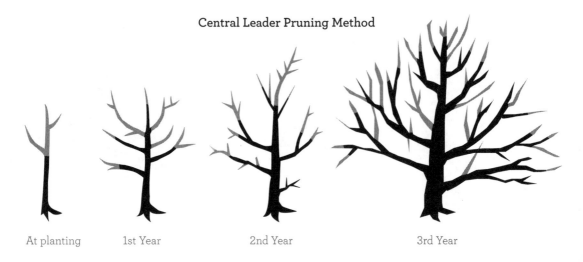

Central Leader Pruning Method

At planting   1st Year   2nd Year   3rd Year

main pruning in the winter so you give energy to the roots by limiting the number of buds for growth in the spring and do a light pruning in the summer to help control size. Others say prune in spring and summer to remove upright shoots and head shoots to control height. Still other experts say to prune many times during the year: in spring prune for shape while the tree is blooming so you can be sure not to prune off the season's fruit, prune right after the nickel-sized fruit has been thinned, and prune again after harvest. The multiseason pruning advocates say that especially fast-growing trees may also need a late pruning in late summer, and finally a light winter pruning can be done for structure and aesthetics.

The experts *do* agree that pruning in the winter dormant season from November to March allows you to see the tree's structure and notice broken, diseased, crossing, or competing branches more easily. They also agree that hard winter pruning can cause the tree to produce too much upright branching, including suckers and watersprouts, leaving little energy for fruit growth and development, but that if your tree only put out a foot or two of growth in the last growing season and you want to encourage new growth, winter pruning is needed.

All the experts have had success with their chosen way of pruning, and your choice will have to do with your goals and observation of your tree. If your tree has only put out a small amount of growth, don't summer prune or summer prune lightly. If it is growing rapidly, summer pruning is essential to control its growth. If you winter prune, do it in late winter or early spring.

THE UNCONTESTED TRUTHS OF PRUNING

Relax. Pruning need not be a scary or guilt-ridden task. Annual pruning is best for the tree and will be easiest for you to maintain the chosen shapes, but if you don't get to it for a year or three, don't fret—all will be fine. Pruning fruit trees is not an exact science, as this chapter shows, but there are some uncontested truths to remember when pruning:

- Remove diseased or broken branches.
- Cut off watersprouts (long shoots arising from the tops of branches).
- Cut off suckers (shoots growing from a tree's root or below graft).
- If two branches are crossing or rubbing, thin out the one that is weakest or most poorly placed.
- Cut out any branches that are crowding each other—usually the lowest one.
- Cut out branches that block sunlight and air circulation.
- Cut out branches to let you have access to the interior to pick the fruit.

In our northernmost regions, any dormant pruning that is done should happen in late winter to help prevent *Pseudomonas syringae* canker infections, which can potentially cause numerous problems on fruit trees if trees are pruned before freezing temperatures occur. If you are pruning to let light into the tree, prune anytime in the growing season, usually May through August. Thinning out suckers or watersprouts in summer gets rid of them before they get too large.

Dozens of wonderful books and videos are available about pruning, and we encourage you to consult them. Look in the Resources section in the back of this book

TRAINING YOUR YOUNG TREE

When you are training your young tree, you want the main scaffolding branches to grow out from the main trunk at a strong angle. A branch growing up at a narrow angle will create a narrow crotch, and narrow crotches will easily break when the tree is older and the branches are loaded with fruit. Creating wide angles also slows the growth of the scaffolding branches. With the open center shape, forty-five degrees is the best angle for a branch to grow out from the tree trunk; up to sixty degrees is acceptable. When pruning for the central leader shape, you'll want the angles to be more open; sixty degrees is what to aim for, but no matter the shape, a more horizontally growing branch will produce more fruit.

To spread the angle of a young branch that you have selected for a scaffolding branch, use spring-type clothespins, toothpicks, or commercial plastic spreaders. Clip the clothespin to the trunk with the long part of the clothespin pressing down on the thin shoot. Toothpicks can also be used to spread the branch from the trunk. Support the small branch as you gently push one end of a pointed toothpick into it. Bend the branch down gently to get the proper angle, and push the other end of the toothpick into the trunk. As the branch grows, it will continue growing in this more lateral position.

This training can be done with any very young shoot that needs to be slightly redirected. Check the angles often to make sure they are still growing the way you want. When the branch is "trained," move the clothespins to the ends of the branches to weigh them down slightly and prevent upward growth. When branches still need training but are too big for a toothpick or a clothespin to have any effect, wooden spreaders can be made with one-inch-square wood that has a finishing nail (a nail with a very small head) driven into each end and used in the same manner as the toothpick. These are commonly made in various lengths up to eighteen inches. Spreaders are left in place until the branches stiffen—usually one to two years and sometimes up to five years.

for some good ones. If you consult several books, you are likely to find differing ideas on what, how much, and when to prune. Give yourself the freedom to cut off some branches and watch what happens. If you cut off the "wrong" branch, the tree will probably put out another branch to take its place and you will have learned something about pruning. The next time you'll learn a different lesson. It's a give-and-take or maybe take-and-give. Even experienced gardeners keep learning from their trees. One gardener tells the story of a busy winter when she forgot to prune her favorite tree—a small, beautiful Pink Pearl apple tree—until late spring when it was already blooming. Even as she was making the cuts, she worried there would be no pink applesauce come summer. To her relief, though, her harvest was completely normal and possibly even larger than with her traditional dormant pruning.

Pruning Evergreen Fruit Trees

Citrus, loquats, and feijoas are all evergreen trees, which *doesn't* mean they don't ever lose leaves. Leaves drop but just not all at once. Evergreen trees need less pruning than deciduous trees. Prune the citrus canopy to let sunlight and air into the tree's center. You can prune citrus back to three main branches growing out from the center of the tree and leave the smaller, fruit-bearing branches on these main branches. With an open shape, it will be easier to pick the fruit and make harvesting easier. Feijoas can be kept small and compact, large and loose, or sheared like a hedge. Loquats do best with hard or frequent pruning, both to control size and to reduce the number of shoots on the ends of branches.

The Espalier Technique

Espalier describes the art of training a tree to grow in a flat manner, usually on a wire, trellis, fence, wall, or building. The training can be as simple as a trunk with extremely short branches looking like a pole or as complex as several trees crossing in diamond patterns. The shapes can be precise and evenly spaced or free-form. Espalier is a perfect solution for growing trees in small, narrow, or awkward spaces or just for the interest and beauty they provide. We have included a few of the shapes easiest to form or maintain. Apple, pear, citrus, loquat, and fig are good choices for all of the following shapes. Peach, nectarine, plum, and apricot are best suited to the fan shape.

HORIZONTAL CORDON. Most people in the United States think of an espaliered tree as a single trunk with two to three branches growing out horizontally in one plane on each side of the tree because this is the most common form. Young trees already trained in this way are often available from nurseries or by mail. The branches will need something to grow on to help support the heavy fruit. If you are not growing the horizontally espaliered tree along an existing rigid fence, you'll need to create a support system with ten- or twelve-gauge wire stretched securely between strong posts that are firmly secured in the ground. If you will grow your tree along a wall or building, attach the wire using spacers so that each hook is set out from the wall at least two inches.

Loosely wind the branches around the wire or attach the branches with loops of cloth strips or stretchy garden tape so when the fruit gets heavy with juice, the horizontal branch will have some help with the weight. The pruning is simple. Prune out every branch that grows out frontward or backward from the scaffolding branches. After harvest, but while the leaves are still on the tree, head back all new branches to three leaves or leaf groups from the scaffolding branch. As always, thin out any shoots that are crowding or crossing.

VERTICAL CORDON AND OBLIQUE CORDON. A tree can be trained to a single trunk with leaves, very short branches, and fruiting spurs growing close to the trunk. The tree can be planted and grown as an upright "pole," but trees are often set in the ground obliquely at a thirty-five-degree angle either alone or in a row of trees thirty inches or so apart to form a living fence. An oblique cordon will need the same wire support as described for a horizontal cordon but attach a length of bamboo or one-by-three strip of wood at the point where you will plant the tree and at the same angle as you want the tree to grow. As it grows, gently tie the young tree to the supporting bamboo or wood strip. At the end of the growing season, prune any upright branches at three leaves or leaf groups from the trunk and

Espalier: Horizontal Cordon

all other branches around the tree to two leaves from the trunk. When the tree is as tall as you want it, thin out any branches growing above this height. Continue pruning in this way even when the tree is established. It is easier to contain the size of an oblique cordon than an upright cordon.

THE STEP-OVER. This is one of the simplest shapes. It is a trunk with two main branches growing in opposite directions. The step-over shape will need a simple support of one main wire supported securely about fifteen inches from the ground. Cut back the newly planted tree to twelve to fifteen inches. Let two branches grow out near the top of the tree opposite each other. Allow them to grow up in a V-shape for the first spring and summer after planting. In the fall gently bend and tie the branches to the wire. Remove all other shoots. Maintain this configuration by thinning out any other branches growing from the trunk and heading back shoots to three leaves or leaf groups on the top of the branch and to two leaves or leaf groups anywhere else.

FAN SHAPE. The fan-shaped tree has a short trunk with rays coming out from it. Often there are five to seven main branches growing out from the trunk like the fingers of your spread-out hand. Usually the tree is grown with supporting wires as for the other shapes, and bamboo or wood strips are attached to the wires in the pattern you want the tree to adopt. As it matures, the

wood or bamboo is removed, leaving the wire frame to continue supporting the main branches. This shape does not have to be a regular fan shape, and it looks great in front of a building. The fan shape is a good structural choice for peach, nectarine, apricot, and plum trees.

From the Spurs Come the Fruit—Some of It

Apple, pear, plum, and cherry trees produce flowers and fruit on spurs, which are short branches that grow off the main branches. Apple and pear spurs look like stubby, wrinkly branches, and they can remain fruitful for more than ten years. Plum spurs look like thin, pointy three- to four-inch-long branches. The Japanese plum and Italian prune plum spurs will live for five to eight years. Peach and nectarine spurs are pale and fuzzy. Spurs of these stone fruits only produce for about three years. Cherry spurs are only an inch or so long, but sweet cherry spurs make cherries for more than ten years. Sour cherry spurs are only fruitful for three to five years.

Take care of your spurs. They need sun and air circulation. If a spur is shaded, it will eventually stop producing. Be careful not to thin or head back a spur. Thinning will eliminate the spur, and if you head it back, it will grow into a non-fruit-bearing branch. But your tree wants to produce fruit, and new spurs are always being produced. Heading back branches that are about the size of a pencil to three leaves in midsummer will help create new fruit spurs.

Simple Grafting

Three friendly work colleagues were proudly talking about their apple trees. One had a Fuji and a Braeburn, another had both Red Delicious and Yellow Delicious trees, and the third had an heirloom Pippin, a Gala, and an odd-shaped little tree of unknown variety that bore unpleasant-tasting fruit. All wanted more apple trees but had no space to grow more. An imaginative member of the trio came up with the idea of trading pruned-off branches to graft them onto other trees. If the grafts worked, the person growing the Fuji could soon, with any luck, have a couple of branches bearing Gala apples on her Fuji tree, a couple more bearing Yellow Delicious, and so on. None of these people had ever tried tree grafting before but figured, how hard could it be? They began a project of learning and attempting to mix and match apple varieties.

Grafting is simply the joining together of two plant parts so that they grow into one. It is most commonplace to graft a pencil-thin fruit tree (scion) to a different root system (rootstock) to get desired

CAN YOU EVER HAVE TOO MUCH FRUIT?

What do you do on the cloudless early summer day when you look out your window and see scores of glistening plums rapidly ripening on the branches, and you are packing to go off for two weeks on a long-awaited trip. You know that upon your return all those plums will be a sodden red mess all over your patio. What to do when your harvest is just too much for you to use or process, or you don't want to pick all those apples way up in the tree, or when all of your friends politely refuse the third or fourth bag of lemons you've offered? Who can you call if you just want to share your fruitful wealth?

You call the gleaners, that's what you do. Gleaning is the act of collecting leftover crops, often nowadays from farms and businesses but also from backyards. There are volunteer gleaning groups in cities big and small. They will come yearly to take away fruit before it drops to the ground or only when you call. A small crew of pickers will come to your home, carefully harvest the fruit you are not going to use, and take it where it will do the most good—usually a local food bank, shelter, or soup kitchen where the fresh fruit is greatly appreciated. If there isn't a group in your area that is able to come to your yard to pick your fruit, any of the organizations above would be thrilled to have fruit delivered to them. It's win-win for everyone. You will be providing a nutritious food to people who need it and preventing possible insect and fungal spread by keeping all the fallen fruit off the ground (or keeping unfallen fruit from mummifying on the tree).

growth and fruiting characteristics. Most of us have seen or heard of trees that have up to six different apple varieties grafted onto one trunk.

It can be a relatively easy and satisfying project to take a branch from your neighbor's (or work friend's) tree and graft it onto your own, and quite possibly have an apple of a new variety grow on your tree the next spring. There are several methods for making the grafting cuts, but they all involve a very sharp knife. (Don't even attempt grafting with a dull knife.) The easiest method of cutting and preparing a tree and branch for their eventual union is the simple whip graft. When the tree is dormant, just before the sap starts, is the best time to do this.

The branch to be grafted (the donor branch) should be very recently clipped off its home tree and kept moist, wrapped tightly, and placed in the refrigerator until you are ready to work with it. Upon receiving the half inch (or smaller) in diameter branch, follow these instructions:

1. Find a branch on your tree that pretty closely matches the donor branch in diameter.

2. Cut it off with clippers, leaving no less than a foot attached to the tree.

3. With the sharp knife, cut the branch again, making a slanted 1- to 1½-inch cut diagonally up the branch. You should be able to accomplish this with a sharp knife in one quick stroke. It's fine to try it again if the cut is not smooth.

4. Next make a similar cut on the donor branch.

5. Match and press the cut sides together, lining up the cambium layers (the thin layer between the bark and the wood). It they don't match exactly because one branch is slightly larger, make sure the cambium layers touch on at least one side.

6. You've come to the tricky part. You have to hold these two sides together while wrapping them firmly with tape. You can buy special grafting tape, but electrical tape works just fine. Start wrapping about an inch below the join and continue for another inch above it.

That's it. The tree will do the rest of the work. Cut or loosen the tape a month or so after the branch has begun growing.

By the way, the work friends mentioned at the beginning of this section all succeeded with at least one graft, but the friend with the odd little tree managed to give the ugly duckling a makeover that turned it into a melting pot of apple trees, producing no fewer than five different varieties each season.

Part II

FAVORITE FRUIT TREES
FOR THE PACIFIC MARITIME CLIMATE

Now we talk about specific trees and fruits and how they grow, including any special considerations you should know about. This is followed by a list of varieties of trees suggested for your zone by the experts. They are loosely ranked in order, with the experts' favorites listed first. Next—and this is the section you will turn to again and again over the years—you will find remarkably delicious fruit recipes used by talented chefs in popular restaurants up and down the Pacific Coast.

By grouping areas with similar average minimum winter temperatures, the USDA Plant Hardiness Zone Map (on page 18) shows three major zones (Zones 8, 9, and 10) that span the regions covered in this book. Zones 8 and 9 are further divided into 8a, 8b, 9a, and 9b sections. Though it is backward alphabetically, we started with Zone 8b to move roughly west to east—left to right on the map. Zone 8 covers the area from southern British Columbia through most of western Oregon, with Zone 8b comprising the most coastal areas and Zone 8a more inland. Zone 9 starts in the westernmost coastal areas of central Oregon and continues south through California. Zone 9b is a thin band starting midway along the Oregon Coast and extending down the length of California; Zone 9a is more inland. Zone 10 is a relatively smaller zone, including the San Francisco Bay region and hugging the coast southward. The trees chosen by horticultural experts for each zone are the ones that fit the zones' growing requirements most closely.

Apple

(Malus domestica)

Not only are apple trees resplendent in the spring with dazzling pink or white flowers, but first-time fruit tree growers will also find that apple trees are some of the most prolific and easiest fruit trees to grow. The apple is one of the hardiest and most widely grown of fruit trees. Thought to hail from what is now Afghanistan and adapted to grow in most temperate regions of the world, an apple tree needs a certain amount of cold or chill time in the winter months to set fruit properly.

The amount of time for each variety is rarely an exact figure, and some apples said to need many chilling hours are being grown successfully in the warm winters of Southern California. Ask your neighbors what has grown well for them. Apples with low chilling hours are available and every bit as tasty as the apples from trees that like a little frostbite.

Standard apple trees can grow to forty feet tall. Some folks who don't want a tree that tall may entertain the idea of a dwarf variety. This might not be the wisest choice, though. Many nurseries recommend a semi-dwarf rootstock that is more tolerant of the region's wet, clay soil than either dwarf varieties or standard ones, but don't be fooled by the word "dwarf" in the term "semi-dwarf." These can grow to thirty feet if not pruned. Some nurseries recommend growing on rootstock from standard-sized trees—if you are committed to summer pruning to keep your tree small—to take advantage of the standard's vigor. Diligent pruning can keep trees to a manageable eight to ten feet and still produce a bountiful amount of apples.

Apple trees are well-suited to pruning to the central leader shape described in chapter 3, "Pruning Deciduous Fruit Trees," but they are just as easily trained to the open center shape or as fruit bushes. Compared to other varieties of fruit trees, apples are easy to espalier. Apple trees lend well to this artistic and space-saving option because their branches are sturdy and can tolerate physical manipulation without much risk of being broken. Columnar apple trees are another space-saving option home gardeners can consider. Relatively new on the market, these trees have been hybridized to grow straight up to nine feet with little or no branching. They almost look like the old-fashioned barbershop poles, except instead of stripes there are apples staggered around the trunk. Columnar trees are quite a conversation piece with their almost modelesque statures. One can be tucked into a very small space, or several can be grouped together in a tiny grove.

Apple flowers and fruit are borne on spurs, short stubs of branches that look crinkled because of the closely spaced ridges going around them. Spurs are important to identify because you don't want to cut them off in your winter pruning thinking that they are branches, which will seriously reduce the size of your harvest. Apple spurs can produce apples for more than ten years. Some apple varieties need another apple tree in the area to provide cross-pollination, while others can pollinate themselves and thrive even if there is only one apple tree on the block. Experts say that all apple varieties do best with another apple tree nearby, however. You don't need to buy more than one tree for your yard if you live in a dense urban area with lots of backyard fruit trees. If you live in an area with little vegetation or a more rural area, you will want to take two little trees home with you from the nursery. Make sure that they are trees that produce pollen and have the same blooming time.

Not all apple trees can pollinate other apple trees. If you are depending on two apple trees to pollenize each other, make sure they both produce fertile pollen. Jonathan, Mutzu, Gravenstein, and Winesap are examples of apples that cannot provide pollen for other trees.

To ensure quality fruit of good size, it is wise to thin the young apples when they are about nickel-sized. If a fruit tree has flowered profusely, it sometimes has a normal fruit drop to protect itself from the strain of trying to nourish a huge crop through maturity. After the tree drops some fruit (or sometime in June if it hasn't), it's your turn. Thin apples by cutting or twisting off all but one little apple per cluster. It might be painful to think of removing all those baby apples, but by thinning them, you will get larger apples and you won't have to worry about branches breaking due to the weight of too much juicy fruit.

Harvest time for apples in Pacific maritime regions can range from July through

November. When you pick an apple, don't pull it quickly downward or you may damage the spur, which will limit its ability to produce fruit in that spot in the following year. Instead, twist the apple upward. Many apple varieties keep well for several months in a cool place. Some of the most highly valued heirloom varieties were the "good keepers" able to retain their taste and texture for the longest time. Gardeners report being able to store their Granny Smith apples up to ten months in the basement to provide crunchy apples almost all year long. The flavor of some apples, like the Cox's Pippin, improves and gets more complex with storage. Wrapping each perfect apple—blemishes that break the skin will cause the fruit to spoil more quickly—in a layer of tissue or newspaper to keep the apples from touching is a good idea. One thing to keep in mind when storing apples is to keep them away from other fruits because the apples emit ethylene, which speeds the ripening (and spoiling) of other fruits and vegetables.

CUTTING AND PEELING GADGET

Once your apple trees are in full production and you're ready to make all sorts of wonderful pies and crisps, you may wish you had a little help with the cutting and peeling. You could put your family members to work with knives and cutting boards, but an easier option might be to borrow or purchase an apple corer/peeler/slicer—a hand-cranked little gadget that will have your kids (or other adults) more than happy to help. Some styles clamp to the table with a vacuum base, and others clamp to the edge of a table or cutting board. An apple is pushed onto the end prongs and twirled through the stainless-steel corer while the knife edge on the side slices the apple in a continuous spiral. The attached peeler digs in to follow the contour of the apple and efficiently remove the peel.

Little can go wrong with this nifty device and you will be using it for years. The peelings come off in long continuous strips that kids love to eat or play with. Hold a strip up in the air with one arm and try to catch the other end in your mouth to eat, like a very long spaghetti noodle. If you decide not to eat the peels, throw a peeling over your shoulder and see what letter it forms. It is said that it will form the initial of the person you will marry. (If you don't like the way it comes out, toss another one!)

Best Bets for Apples

The following lists tell which apples are suited to their respective zones. There are likely many more that would grow well in each zone; however, these varieties are the ones that experts most highly recommend.

BEST BETS FOR ZONE 8B

AKANE. Also called Tokyo Rose, this excellent dessert apple is sweet spicy, with a complex flavor and aroma. Ideal in coastal climates especially in inclement springs, it is an extremely reliable August bearer, with mixed reviews on storage, but it keeps well on the tree. Disease resistant. Needs a pollenizer.

LIBERTY. This variety is like a McIntosh with tarter flavor and crisper flesh. When picked fully ripe, it has the flavor suggestive of freshly squeezed apple cider. A heavy bearer and one of the most disease-resistant varieties. Thin fruit clusters to one apple per spur to get the best size and quality. Self-fertile.

PRISTINE. A golden-yellow variety with a smooth glossy skin, the Pristine ripens in early July. It is mildly tart but high in sugar content, with excellent keeping quality for an early-season variety. The tree is vigorous and disease resistant. Needs a pollenizer.

ENTERPRISE. A brilliantly glossy dark-red apple with firm, crispy, somewhat spicy-tasting flesh, this is a good choice for eating out of hand or cooking. It is a newer vigorous, disease-resistant variety. The apples will store for four to six months with a slight increase in intensity of flavor. Ripens in mid-October. Needs a pollenizer.

WILLIAM'S PRIDE. A very disease-resistant variety with excellent rich, spicy flavor that has a long harvesting season but short storage time. With dark-red stripes on a green-yellow background, these abundant apples need to be thinned early and heavily so the branches are not overloaded. Needs a pollenizer.

BEST BETS FOR ZONE 8A

WYNOOCHEE EARLY. This beautiful tree bears crisp and flavorful large fruit that is creamy yellow with red stripes. Ripens in late July or early August. It is unusual in that it is an early variety that stores well. You could still be eating these apples at Christmas. Very disease resistant. Needs a pollenizer.

WILLIAM'S PRIDE. A very disease-resistant variety with rich, spicy flavor that has a long picking season but short storage time. Dark-red stripe on a green-yellow background. These productive trees and the apples they produce need to be thinned early and heavily so the branches are not overloaded. Needs a pollenizer.

GRAVENSTEIN. This classic red- and green-striped apple is so juicy that it's hard to keep it from running down your chin. Reliably produces abundant crops for terrific pies and cider. Ripens in July. It can sometimes get scab but still bears well. Needs a pollenizer but cannot pollenize other trees.

ENTERPRISE. This beautiful dark-red apple with firm, crispy, somewhat spicy-tasting flesh is a good choice for eating out of hand or cooking. It's a newer disease-resistant vigorous variety. The apples will store for four to six months with a slight increase in intensity of flavor. Ripens in mid-October. Needs a pollenizer.

HONEYCRISP. Just like the name says, these apples taste honey-sweet, with just a dash of tartness, and have surprising crispness. A great tree for the Northwest, it bears big scarlet-red-over-yellow fruit. Ripens in September and can be stored for three or four months in the refrigerator. Needs a pollenizer.

BEST BETS FOR ZONE 9B

EMPIRE. This is a wonderful midseason tree for this zone. These crisp, juicy apples have dark-red striped skin and a sweet and mildly tart delicious flavor. Good in hot summers as well as in cool coastal climates, this tree bears crops reliably and starts producing at an early age. Needs a pollenizer.

AKANE. Also called Tokyo Rose, it is an excellent dessert apple with sweet spicy, complex flavor and aroma. Ideal in coastal climates especially in inclement springs, it is an extremely reliable August bearer, with mixed reviews on storage, but it keeps well on the tree. Scab and mildew resistant. Needs a pollenizer.

WINTER BANANA. This pretty apple grows best in milder coastal climates. It ripens a little too early inland, and the taste is not as good. These large juicy apples have yellow-blushed pink skin and delicious tangy dessert flavor that keeps well. It has low chill requirements. It is partly self-pollenized, and it is a good pollenizer for other varieties.

LIBERTY. This looks like a McIntosh and has a sweetly tart flavor and crisp flesh. When picked fully ripe, it has the flavor suggestive of freshly squeezed apple cider. A heavy bearer and one of the most disease-resistant varieties. Thin fruit clusters to one apple per spur to get the best size and quality. Ripens late midseason. The tree is productive and the apples keep well. Self-fertile.

WYNOOCHEE EARLY. This beautiful tree bears large crops of crisp and flavorful big fruit that is creamy yellow with red stripes. Ripens in late July or early August. It is unusual in that it is an early variety that stores well. You could still be eating these apples at Christmas. Very disease resistant. Needs a pollenizer.

BEST BETS FOR ZONE 9A

FUJI. Everyone loves the Fuji with its sweet crisp, flavorful taste. Its best flavor comes out with warm autumns, and it ripens in early winter. It needs a pollenizer, and it's an excellent pollenizer for other apples.

PINK LADY. These tangy and sweet medium-sized apples with a pink blush on yellow skin are great for eating out of hand and are perfect for fruit salads since they resist turning brown after cutting and hold their texture and flavor when cooked. They ripen in September and are self-fertile.

MUTSU. A very large, green, somewhat oval apple from Japan, the Mutsu has juicy and crisp flesh, good for fresh eating and great for cooking and baking. It's a good keeper. Needs a pollenizer but cannot pollenize other trees.

ANNA. This apple is bred in Israel, so its winter chill requirement is remarkably low. It has a light greenish-yellow skin with a slight red blush. The flesh is sweet but slightly tart and crispy. Anna blooms early, and the fruit ripens in midsummer. The trees produce at a young age, and the fruit keeps well. Needs a pollenizer.

GALA. One of the best apples for fresh eating, the Gala is a medium-sized orange-red over golden-yellow fruit. Deliciously sweet fruit with a hint of tang, these trees bear prolifically and need heavy thinning (one fruit per cluster) to produce good-sized fruit. Needs a pollenizer.

BEST BETS FOR ZONE 10

GOLDEN DELICIOUS. And they are delicious in this zone! This apple is an old favorite with good reason, and it's even better when homegrown. An excellent apple for the coastal region, it is edible when green and ripens to a mellow flavor when yellow in September. Needs a pollenizer.

FUJI. Everyone loves the Fuji with its sweet crisp, flavorful taste. Its best flavor comes out with warm autumns, and it ripens in early winter. It needs a pollenizer, and it's an excellent pollenizer for other apples.

GRAVENSTEIN. These big crispy juicy, aromatic apples will be the earliest apple treats in your garden. They ripen in July, to eat out of hand or use for juicy sauce or baking. Needs a pollenizer, but cannot pollenize other trees.

PINK PEARL. How about some pink applesauce? The skin of the Pink Pearl is mostly cream and pale green, but the flesh is pink and aromatic. The taste is tart to sweet depending on picking time. An excellent choice for the Pacific maritime climate, this tree has beautiful pink flowers in the spring. Needs a pollenizer.

STAYMAN WINESAP. One of the best tastes imaginable when the fruit is really ripe! Don't pick an apple till it is ready to drop into your hand, and that might not be till Halloween or even Thanksgiving. This is an heirloom variety with a rich winelike flavor and firm, juicy flesh. It produces well in mild coastal climates. Needs a pollenizer but does not pollenize other apples.

Heirloom Apples

Historically apples were bred for specific uses. Apples came to North America with the first European settlers, who used them for sweetener, hard cider, and vinegar. Early settlers established nurseries and orchards wherever they moved. Varieties were chosen for propagation through grafting, based on the use to which they would be put. Any of these varieties whose apples were "good keepers" were doubly prized. The apple varieties available in most grocery stores today are bred for their ability to be mechanically harvested, their storability, and their resistance to bruising in transit. In an average store that means six to eight varieties are for sale, and most of these are offered for fresh eating.

We are lucky that many of the best of the old varieties are still being grown and sold through specialty nurseries. Some nurseries, historical museums, and farmers markets will offer samples in the fall so you can taste some of the venerable varieties. You very well may fall in love with more than one. Planting an heirloom apple preserves a bit of history, and you also may discover flavor complexity you didn't know could come from an apple.

Best Bets for Heirloom Apples

Because many of the older apple varieties were grown for cooking, but we also love to be able to eat an apple out of hand, most of the apples on this list combine the best of both of these attributes. All of these varieties either require or produce better with another tree for pollination.

BEST BET FOR ZONE 8B

EGREMONT RUSSET. A classic russet apple that's very popular in the United Kingdom, this apple has a rich, nutty flavor that gets drier in storage and the taste becomes somewhat pear-like. It is delicious in salads and with cheese. It has rough greenish-yellow skin with golden-brown and darker-brown patches.

BEST BET FOR ZONE 8A

WICKSON CRABAPPLE. A very sweet apple originally grown for cider, this is still a popular juice and cider apple because of its balanced sweetness, tang, and spice. This tree bears an impressively abundant crop of small red-and-yellow apples that are as prized for their delicious taste right off the tree as for their cider.

BEST BET FOR ZONE 9B

NORTHFIELD BEAUTY. This one likes to grow in cooler regions and doesn't like the heat. It ripens in the same season as the Gravenstein but doesn't drop fruit prematurely. In fact, don't wait for this fruit to fall—it will hang on the tree looking red and beautiful till it's mushy. It is very resistant to the apple scab fungus. The Northfield Beauty may be better for cooking than for fresh eating.

BEST BETS FOR ZONE 9A

WALTANA. This variety does best with a long hot growing season and ripens in late October or November. Some say its best flavor develops after a frost. A great keeper, a Waltana can be stored for six months or more. It has a good sweet–tart balance and is used for fresh eating as well as juice, hard cider, cooking, and desserts.

WHITE ASTRACHAN. Pale greenish skin with a red blush and white freckles characterizes this variety. Crisp, juicy, and tart, it's great for eating out of hand or for cooking, cider, and applesauce, but the White Astrachan is not a good keeper. This one is good for inland areas because its heavy foliage protects the fruit from sunburn.

BEST BET FOR ZONE 10

The famous French nurseryman Georges Delbard said about the Freyberg: "a veritable cocktail of flavors with the merest touch of anise and producing a juice that combines the taste of apple, pear, and banana." How can you go wrong?

FREYBERG. This is a hybrid of Cox's Pippin and Golden Delicious. It has a lot of the aroma and flavor of the Pippin with the sweetness and juicy crispness of a Golden Delicious. It has green-yellow skin, and it's a good keeper.

BEATING THE TREES: WASSAILING CEREMONIES

Wassailing the fruit orchard—toasting to the health of the orchard with hard cider—was a traditional folk custom in England. People in the cider- and perry-making regions held themselves responsible for both awakening the fruit trees from their midwinter's slumber and driving off any malevolent spirits that might be lurking about the orchard. For this serious yet merry chore, they brought along pots, drums, whistles, and all manner of noise-makers. They also brought along bread and bowls of cider made from the orchard's bounty.

The villagers praised the trees' fruitfulness in the year past with songs, poetry, and speeches and then exhorted them with more rhymes and speeches to bear plentifully in the coming year. According to some accounts of the ritual, when the speeches came to an end, the hitting of the tree trunks and low branches with sticks began. Although it seems like a jarring and unfriendly follow-up to all the praise, it was thought that pounding would help with the wake-up call and put the sap on notice that it would soon be time to rise. After the beating came more toasting and then the drinking of the cider. The trees were ceremonially invited to partake, as people placed cider-soaked bread in low branches and forks in the trees to give thanks to the tree spirits. More cider was sprinkled on the ground around the trees and shared among the human participants in honor of the trees.

From our twenty-first-century vantage point, we can wonder if the apple growers of yore knew that codling moth larvae were tucked away under loose bits of bark awaiting their own spring awakening. The sticks hitting the tree trunks would certainly dislodge or crush a portion of the moth population thereby contributing to the health of the next year's crop. We probably will never know if this was part of the motivation for the hitting, but why not? The ancient growers were well versed in grafting and budding, and practicing methods of insect control could very well have been within their realm of knowledge.

With cider brews regaining popularity, there has been a small resurgence of orchard wassailing ceremonies in the United Kingdom, the United States, and Canada held on the traditional wassailing evening of old Twelfth Night (January 17). A wassail queen or king often leads the procession to the orchard, and there are usually bonfires and sometimes marshmallows, but there is always noise and songs, and there is always cider, both hard and sweet.

THE GLORIOUS APPLE HARVEST

Applesauce, fritters, pie, and Waldorf salad are all classic apple dishes, but apples are so versatile. They can be mixed with grains or vegetables, as in an apple and quinoa cobbler, apple-potato salad, or squash-apple soup. Or try a cheddar and apple frittata. Even a young child can learn to create a scrumptious apple crumble, and kids love dried apples in their lunches. When you need a quick, last-minute dessert, whole apples baked with maple syrup and nuts is an easy and winning option.

CURED HERRING WITH GRANNY SMITH APPLES, RED ONIONS, AND CORIANDER

A Scandinavian favorite, cured (or pickled) herring deserves to be better known. Vancouver chef Frank Pabst of Blue Water Cafe + Raw Bar offers a creamy, not-too-sweet version that is sure to win converts, with finely diced fish accented by crisp, tart apple. Of course, adding savory onion beignets to the plate doesn't hurt. MAKES 4 SERVINGS

2 cups water

¼ cup salt

1 tablespoon sugar

4 frozen herrings, thawed and scaled

2 Granny Smith apples

2 tablespoons sour cream

1 tablespoon plain yogurt

1 tablespoon mayonnaise

Juice of 1 lemon

1 tablespoon chopped fresh dill

1 tablespoon chopped fresh chives

Salt and pepper

In a medium saucepan, combine the water, salt, and sugar and bring to a boil on high heat. Remove from the heat, allow to cool, then refrigerate the brine until ready to use.

Using a sharp knife, make an incision behind either side of the head on each herring to expose the spine. Place the herring on its back then pull the head slowly upward and toward the tail. This way you should be able to pull out most of the tiny bones, although you will likely never get them all. Cut out the fins, then cut the fillets from the bones and debone the flesh as much as possible. Discard the heads, spines, and fins. Place the fillets in the cold brine for 1 hour, then lay them out on a dry towel and scrape off most of the skin. Cut the herring fillets into ¼-inch dice. Reserve a few pieces for garnish.

Peel and core one apple and cut it into ¼-inch dice. Core the remaining apple, then julienne on a mandoline or using a sharp knife.

1 tablespoon coriander seeds,
   toasted and crushed
2 tablespoons finely diced
   red onion
1 bunch baby watercress,
   rinsed and patted dry, plus
   a few sprigs for garnish
2 tablespoons walnut oil
Dash of sherry vinegar

ONION BEIGNETS
4 cups canola oil
   (for deep-frying)
¼ cup tempura flour
¼ cup ice-cold water
½ small onion, cut into
   8 thin rings
4 slices pumpernickel bread

In a small bowl stir together the sour cream, yogurt, mayonnaise, lemon juice, dill, and chives. Season to taste with salt and pepper. Add the coriander seeds, red onion, diced apple, and herring. In a separate bowl toss the julienned apple with the watercress, walnut oil, and sherry vinegar.

Just before serving the cured herring, make the ONION BEIGNETS. Heat the canola oil to 350 degrees F in a deep fryer or heavy pot with high sides. In a small bowl, combine the tempura flour and water until just mixed. There will still be small lumps in the batter. Dip the onion rings in the batter, then fry for 1 minute or until golden brown. Remove from the oil and allow them to drain on several layers of paper towel. Season with salt.

To serve, on each of four plates, arrange a quarter of the cured fish in a line. Top with the reserved herring pieces and the apple salad. Arrange watercress mixture around the plate and serve with a slice of pumpernickel bread and two onion beignets.

FILET MIGNON WITH APPLE–CHESTNUT DRESSING

Here's one for date night. This classy steak dinner for two, from Chef Lisa Scott Owens of Olympia's The Mark Restaurant, offers a savory outlet for your dried apples, the sweet fruit balancing the nutty chestnuts, with the prosciutto's salty edge rounding out the flavors. Chef Owens recommends sourcing organic and local products for superior flavor and the best nutritional value, not only for the produce but for your beef as well. MAKES 2 SERVINGS

Recipe Note: You can use jarred chestnuts that come already peeled, but if you can find them fresh in the market, peel your own. Begin by cutting an X in the end of the chestnut with a sharp knife. Heat a sauté pan as hot as you can and roast them until brown. Let them cool slightly, then slip off the shells.

Two 8-ounce filets mignon

½ cup plus 2 tablespoons extra-virgin olive oil

Sea salt and freshly cracked black pepper

Approximately 2 dried apples, chopped into small bits

12 peeled chestnuts, halved

2 ounces prosciutto di Parma

1 bunch fresh spinach, rinsed, dried, and stems trimmed

½ teaspoon fennel seeds

Preheat the oven to 150 degrees F. Rub the steaks with ½ tablespoon of olive oil and season with sea salt and cracked black pepper on both sides. Set aside.

Place the dried apples on a baking sheet and heat in the oven for about 15 minutes, to remove any excess moisture. Remove the apples and place in a food processor. Chop finely and set aside.

In a small skillet, cook and stir the chestnuts over medium-high heat in ½ cup of the olive oil until lightly colored. Add the chopped apples and prosciutto, stirring to heat through. Drop in a pinch of sea salt as needed, and turn the heat to low. Raise the oven temperature to 375 degrees F.

Heat an ovenproof sauté pan over high and add 1 tablespoon of the olive oil. When the oil is hot, carefully sear each steak for approximately 3 minutes on each side. Place the pan in the oven and roast until done, about 7 or 8 minutes for medium rare and not more than 10 minutes total. Remove the steaks and place on a plate to rest.

While the steaks settle, steam the spinach in a covered saucepan for 5 minutes, then strain the moisture. Heat the remaining olive oil in another sauté pan and stir in the fennel seeds. Add the spinach and toss to coat, seasoning with salt.

To serve, divide the spinach between two plates, creating a flat bed, then place the steaks on top. Pour the apple–chestnut dressing over the steaks, cascading onto the plates.

APPLE-CINNAMON SCONES WITH MAPLE GLAZE

These ethereal scones from Heather Earnhardt of Seattle's Volunteer Park Café offer the concentrated flavor and texture of dried apples, all topped with a luscious maple glaze. A wonderful way to start a weekend morning, they would be just at home with a mug of tea on a chilly fall day. Before you begin, make sure your butter is super cold to ensure the scones are light and flaky. **MAKES 1 DOZEN**

SCONES

3 cups unbleached
    all-purpose flour
2 tablespoons granulated
    sugar
1 teaspoon kosher salt
1 teaspoon freshly ground
    cinnamon
1 cup dried Malcoun or
    Gravenstein apples
    (or similar type), cut
    into chunks
2½ sticks (1¼ cups) butter,
    diced and then frozen
    for 20 minutes
3 eggs
¾ cup heavy cream
1 tablespoon vanilla extract

MAPLE GLAZE

1 cup confectioners' sugar,
    sifted
2 tablespoons pure maple
    syrup

Preheat the oven to 375 degrees F.

Sift together the flour, granulated sugar, salt, and cinnamon in a large bowl. Toss with the dried apples and transfer to a freestanding electric mixer. With the mixer running on low speed, add the butter and mix until the butter pieces are the size of dimes.

In a medium bowl, whisk together the eggs, heavy cream, and vanilla extract. Add to the flour mixture. Be careful to mix just to incorporate; overworking the dough will result in tough scones.

Immediately turn out the dough onto a floured surface. Pat the dough into a circle about 2 inches thick. Cut into rounds with a biscuit cutter or glass and place the rounds on a baking sheet. Brush the rounds with heavy cream and sprinkle with a little granulated sugar.

Put in the oven and bake for 15 minutes or until golden brown. While the scones are baking, whisk together the confectioners' sugar and maple syrup in a small bowl. Drizzle the MAPLE GLAZE over the warm scones and enjoy while they're hot!

HARD APPLE CIDER

To make hard cider, you can use an apple specifically grown for cider or a combination of several apple varieties. You'll want a balanced blend of sweet, tart, and bitter flavors. Winesap is an old cider-making favorite and Waltana is a newer variety with sufficient flavor for great cider. Wickerson crabapple can add an important full-bodied tannic element. Amere De Berthcourt is another of the best varieties for hard cider or added to a sweet cider to give it some spice. As in so many things, there is not just one way to make hard cider. Recipes and methods abound. We have included a basic description of the process, but we definitely encourage you to do more research before embarking on the hard cider voyage. The most recommended and widely available book for beginners is *Cider* by Annie Proulx and Lew Nichols. For hands-on experience, look for classes on brewing and cider making or find a cider mentor.

Making hard cider from apple juice is done simply by adding yeast to change the apple sugars to alcohol. You can make hard cider the way it has been made for centuries—straight from the press—or start with juice that has been pasteurized to kill any bacteria. If you don't pasteurize the juice, the cider will be fermented by wild yeasts present on the apples or in the air as well as any yeasts you may add. The flavor will probably be different than if you started with pasteurized juice. It might be better and it might not, as there is no way to tell what wild yeasts are floating around. It is your choice, of course, but most commercial brewers start with pasteurized cider. (If you start with a commercial apple juice, make sure it has no added preservatives.) You will need:

- juice that has been simmered for about forty-five minutes if you have decided to pasteurize
- yeast (champagne yeast is often used) from a home-brewing store
- sanitizing solution to clean all containers, spoons, and so on (use a capful of bleach in water or a no-rinse sanitizer from a home-brewing store)
- a glass jug
- a rubber stopper and airlock
- a rubber tube for siphoning

- bottles and bottle caps
- granulated or brown sugar, honey, or raisins (all optional—
  use this extra sugar if you want a more alcoholic cider)

If you are adding sugar, do it while the juice is still hot so it can dissolve, and then let the juice cool. While you are waiting for the juice to cool, wash with soapy water and then sanitize the glass jug, stopper, and airlock—anything that will come in contact with the cider. When the juice is almost room temperature, pour it into the jug up to the neck—don't overfill—and stir in the yeast. Seal the jug with the airlock so the carbon dioxide produced by the conversion of sugar to alcohol can escape but air or other bacteria can't get in. (If air does get in, your end product will resemble vinegar more than cider.)

Put the jug in a dark place that is between 60 and 70 degrees Fahrenheit for two weeks to two months. It will bubble, and toward the end of two weeks or so, the bubbling will slow, signaling the end of the primary fermentation process. With the rubber tube, siphon the cider from the jar to another sanitized container, but don't let the tube go into the sludge at the bottom. That sludge is a good addition for your compost.

Rinse the original glass jug and pour the decanted cider back in, cork it again with the airlock, and let it age for another week to twelve days. Bottle it in sanitized bottles. You can reuse soda bottles, or if you think you will make more cider next year, buy some nice bottles at the home-brewing store. The last step is to let the sealed bottles sit at room temperature for a couple of days, then put them in the refrigerator to stop the fermentation process. For a harder (more alcoholic) cider, let it age longer. Hard cider is more like wine than like beer, and the flavor will improve, up to a point, as it ages.

5

Citrus

(Citrus)

The dazzlingly shiny green foliage of a citrus tree is enough to seduce anyone to take one home for display in the yard or for that sunniest spot in the living room—or both. Since citrus are evergreen subtropical plants, they need no chilling time. Although they generally are thought of as hot weather trees, a few are happy in our maritime climate. Most need more pampering than other kinds of fruit trees, however.

All of the citrus trees have to be protected from frost, and most need significant heat to produce well. Few will survive through the winter outside in the northern coastal Zone 8b except the cold-hardy Meyer lemon if it is in that perfect spot.

In most of the coastal region's zones, citrus trees are most likely to thrive in the full sun and when they are near a wall that provides radiant heat. There are many reports of happy lemons and limes, but a few gardeners also have contentedly fruitful oranges in the ground in Zones 9 and 10 away from the coast. Especially when they are young, citrus trees need to be covered or, if in pots, moved inside when frost hits. Make sure the covering doesn't touch the leaves.

All Meyer trees sold today are the dwarf variety and grow to ten feet or so, but they can be kept smaller by pruning and can still produce more than enough fruit for a sizable family. The Meyer is sweeter and less acidic than the Eureka, which is the common grocery-store lemon. The Eureka grown in the ground is taller and has a wider spread than the Meyer. In Zone 8, just like the Meyer, your Eureka may have to be grown in a deep pot and spend the winter in a sunny spot in your house. But don't worry about fitting a tree through the door, as it will only grow to about five feet when grown in a pot.

Most people consider the seedless Bearss lime to be the best true lime. The Rangpur lime is actually a bitter orange. Both of these limes can do well in pots. Mandarin oranges in Zone 10 are reported to have excellent flavor, but they are sometimes susceptible to fire blight. This condition is unsightly but doesn't seem to limit the quality or quantity of the harvest. Although you might need to prune often to keep lemon trees from becoming too dense or tall, other citrus doesn't need much pruning unless you want to thin or shape the tree. Be sure to snip off the vigorous suckers that grow from the rootstock below the graft before they get too thick. Sometimes lemon trees, which bear at the ends of branches, can bear so heavily the branches break. Head back branches to one-third to one-half their length to strengthen them. Citrus are best pruned before they blossom and after they bear fruit—usually between March and August. Take out any weak or crossing branches. Don't forget your heavy gloves because most kinds of citrus sport healthy thorns.

Espaliering citrus trees is a great space saver, and training a citrus against a warm, south-facing wall can have the added benefit of giving your tree that extra warmth it needs to produce sweet fruit. Expect prolific harvests from your mature lemon and lime trees. In fact, in some areas lemons can be like zucchini in August—you can't even give them away—so it is great that citrus can be stored right on the tree for quite a while. Even when they drop off, you can bring them in and put them in a bowl or on the counter for a few days and in a cool, dark place for a few days more. If you want to keep them longer, put them in the crisper section or in a mesh or perforated bag in the refrigerator where they will keep for several weeks. Avoid using airtight containers, which could collect moisture and cause spoilage.

Best Bets for Citrus

The following lists tell which citrus trees are suited to their respective zones. There are likely more that would grow well in each zone; however, these varieties are the ones that experts most highly recommend.

BEST BETS FOR ZONES 8B AND 8A

Citrus is an iffy proposition for the northern maritime regions. You can try growing an Improved Meyer lemon tree on the warm side of the house under an eave where it doesn't get too wet, but citrus in Zones 8a and 8b really thrives only when grown on very dwarf rootstock in containers and brought inside to a sunny room in the winter when the temperature falls below 50 degrees Fahrenheit. The shiny evergreen leaves are beautiful in their own right, but what could be better than the fragrance of citrus flowers in your house in January? Since you undoubtedly have few flying insects overwintering in your house, citrus flowering in the winter means you will need to have to act as a pollinator by brushing or dabbing with a small soft brush or cotton ball to distribute pollen from flower to flower. If you're ready for the pleasure and commitment, the following trees are suggested:

IMPROVED MEYER LEMON. Just the smell of Meyer lemons sitting in a bowl is reason enough to grow them. They can produce aromatic, waxy, white blossoms and fruit all year long. The sunshine-yellow Meyer is very juicy and a little sweeter and less acidic than other lemons. Very productive. Self-fertile.

WASHINGTON NAVEL ORANGE. This seedless, sweet navel is the hardiest orange. The oranges will be full size even though the tree is small. The fruit will ripen in the winter. Just think about going into your kitchen some midwinter day to pick an orange for breakfast. Self-fertile.

MANDARIN SATSUMA. A little more cold hardy than other citrus, this one can be left out longer than the other citrus in Zone 8 and, if the weather is very mild, possibly all winter. The delicately sweet and delicious, deep-orange fruit is easy to peel and ripens before Christmas. Self-fertile.

BEST BETS FOR ZONE 9B

IMPROVED MEYER LEMON. Classic coastal variety hardy to 18 degrees Fahrenheit on the northern California coast. Doesn't need a lot of heat to ripen. They can produce beautiful, waxy white blossoms and fruit all year long, and both are highly aromatic. The sunshine-yellow Meyer is juicy and a little sweeter and less acidic than other lemons. Very productive. Grows in coastal as well as inland areas. Self-fertile.

SHANGJUAN. This is a cold-tolerant Pummelo-cross citrus that is hardy down to 5 to 10 degrees Fahrenheit. It ripens as early as October and produces a large yellow fruit with good flavored juice that can be used like lemon juice or eaten like a grapefruit (with maybe a little sugar added) when fully ripe. Very productive and ornamental. Self-fertile.

CALAMONDIN. This is another cold-hardy and spectacular mandarin orange–type plant whose abundant, one inch in diameter fruit can be used like lemons or limes even though it looks like an orange. The trees bloom all year long with a wonderful citrus fragrance. Excellent for containers. Self-fertile.

BEARSS LIME. The classic lime taste! This one is best in containers in the coastal areas. It can be grown outside but needs to be protected as it is particularly susceptible to frost. Produces abundant fragrant blossoms, thorns, and greenish-yellow seedless, juicy fruits. Self-fertile.

PIXIE MANDARIN. This variety of mandarin needs the least heat and is the best choice for coastal areas. It has a sweet flavor and it's seedless and easy to peel. The upright and vigorous tree produces lots of medium-small fruits. Self-fertile.

BEST BETS FOR ZONE 9A

Any of the citrus in Zone 9b will grow well in Zone 9a, and you can add these:

EUREKA. This is the lemon you usually see sold commercially. It is thick skinned and will produce a moderate amount of juice used in both sweet and savory dishes. It is easy to espalier and has fewer thorns than most lemon varieties. Self-fertile.

WASHINGTON NAVEL ORANGE. This popular sweet, juicy, seedless variety bears heavily. The fruit has thick, rough, bright orange, easy-to-peel skin, and the segments separate easily. The fruit ripens from fall through winter but can hang on the tree for three to four months. Self-fertile.

CARA CARA ORANGE. This navel orange has a sweet, mildly acidic, berry-like flavor and surprisingly bright pink to red flesh that makes a beautifully colored juice. It is sometimes called Red Navel, and it ripens from fall to winter. Self-fertile.

OWARI SATSUMA MANDARIN ORANGE. This tree has a spreading habit and fragrant flowers. The fruit is seedless, flavorful, and easy to peel. The Satsuma is hardy to 20 degrees Fahrenheit and ripens to a beautiful light orange in the winter. Self-fertile.

KUMQUATS (MEIWA AND NAGANI). Kumquats look like tiny, oval oranges and have edible thick, sweet skin and tangy flesh. Eat the fruit in one bite or slice it into salads. These naturally small trees will only grow two or three feet tall and are very ornamental with their numerous bright orange fruit and shiny dark leaves. Self-fertile.

BEST BETS FOR ZONE 10

IMPROVED MEYER LEMON. This classic coastal variety hardy to 18 degrees Fahrenheit on the Northern California coast doesn't need a lot of heat to ripen. Meyers can produce beautiful, waxy white blossoms and fruit all year long, and both are highly aromatic. The sunshine-yellow Meyer is juicy and a little sweeter and less acidic than other lemons. Very productive. Self-fertile.

EUREKA. This is the lemon you usually see sold commercially. It is thick skinned and will produce a moderate amount of juice used in both sweet and savory dishes. It is easy to espalier and has fewer thorns than most lemon varieties. Self-fertile.

PIXIE MANDARIN. This variety of mandarin needs the least heat and is the best choice for coastal areas. Sweet flavor, seedless, and easy to peel. The upright and vigorous tree produces lots of medium to small fruits. Self-fertile.

SANJUINELLI BLOOD ORANGE. This late-midseason blood orange does well in that very warm spot. The tree is small to medium in size, spineless, and bears an abundant crop. It matures in February but remains fresh and tasty hanging on the tree till April. Self-fertile.

NAGAMI KUMQUAT. Looking like a tiny, oval orange, this kumquat has edible thick, sweet skin and tangy flesh. Eat it in one bite or slice it into salads. This naturally small tree will only grow two to three feet tall and is very ornamental with its numerous bright orange fruit and shiny dark leaves. Self-fertile.

CLEANING WITH CITRUS

We all know how great citrus is for juicing, marinades, and bringing out the flavors in seafood and baked goods, or just eating fresh out of hand. But there are so many other uses for citrus around the house. Cleaning with citrus, especially lemon, is a green way to clean that elevates your mood with the fresh fragrance while you work. Lemon can disinfect, bleach, cut grease, and remove stains. Here are some other great ways to use citrus for cleaning:

- Grind half a lemon through the garbage disposal to leave your kitchen smelling fresh.
- Add lemon juice to a wash cycle to help brighten whites.
- Mix lemon juice, vinegar, and water together for an all-purpose cleaning solution.
- Combine one part lemon juice and two parts olive oil to make quality natural furniture polish.
- Make an easy air freshener by mixing lemon juice and water in a spray bottle.
- Clean and disinfect a cutting board by rubbing a cut lemon into the surface.
- Boil a few lemon peels in water in a blackened pot for 5 to 10 minutes, and after it cools, you'll be able to easily wash the pot.
- To clean the microwave, boil 4 tablespoons of lemon juice and a cup of water in the microwave for 5 minutes. Remove the bowl, and while you are wiping off the condensed moisture from the inside of the microwave, the grease will come off too.

THE GLORIOUS CITRUS HARVEST

When you need a lemon for a recipe or to alleviate a sore throat, there is nothing finer than walking outside to pick this fruit known for its culinary and medicinal gifts. The culinary uses of the lemon seem endless. Kids love lemon bars and lemon cakes. Citrus can add sweetness or zing to your marmalades, sorbets, salads, or salsas. Imagine a lime tart with a lemon crust, or a kumquat and butter lettuce salad. Broiled salmon with orange rounds is just right any evening, and savory lemon rice is the perfect side for spicy chicken. You can freeze sweetened juice in ice cube trays to save for "instant" lemonade or limeade on a hot day. Lemons and limes also make a beautiful and aromatic display just piled in a bowl in the living room. Now, just pull one out whenever you need a lemon for a cup of tea, or a lime for that margarita.

OLIVE OIL-POACHED CALIFORNIA HALIBUT WITH SALSIFY AND MEYER LEMON–MINT RELISH

Because they are less tart and acidic than traditional supermarket varieties, Meyer lemons are often thought of for sweet preparations. But their complex flavor and glorious fragrance work to the same advantage when paired with a lean, mild fish like California halibut, as in this lovely winter dish by Thomas McNaughton of San Francisco's Flour + Water. Chef McNaughton layers the flavor by using Meyer lemon first in an herb crust that covers the fish, then again to scent the poaching oil in which the halibut bathes. Meyer lemon also features in a sprightly relish with mint that adds a bright counterpoint to the silken fish. Though there may seem like a lot of steps, they come together easily in a luscious dish that makes excellent use of the surfeit of lemons from your tree! **MAKES 4 SERVINGS**

    Recipe Note: *Salsify is a fall-harvest root vegetable sometimes called the "oyster plant" because of its flavor, resting somewhere between artichoke and oyster. Long, slow cooking renders both the salsify and the fish tender and luscious. When buying olive oil for poaching, Chef McNaughton advises sparing your pocketbook and choosing pure olive oil. The nuances of extra-virgin would be lost here.*

HALIBUT AND CRUST

½ cup chopped fresh chervil
  leaves

¼ cup chopped fresh tarragon
  leaves

¼ cup chopped fresh mint
  leaves

2 tablespoons Meyer lemon
  zest, finely chopped

Roughly 2 pounds California
  halibut fillet

2 bunches Bloomsdale
  spinach, carefully rinsed,
  dried, and stemmed

SALSIFY AND
POACHING LIQUID

3 Meyer lemons

½ gallon water

6 stalks of salsify

Reserved herb stems
  (from the halibut crust)

2 fresh bay leaves

1 tablespoon black
  peppercorns

3 quarts pure olive oil

Up to two hours before cooking, chop the chervil, tarragon, and
  mint separately with a sharp knife. Reserve the herb stems to
  flavor your poaching oil. In a small bowl, combine the herbs
  with the lemon zest and set aside.

To trim the halibut fillets of all skin and connective tissue place
  the fish skin side down on a cutting board. Insert a sharp, thin
  blade between the skin and the flesh. Gently running the knife
  parallel to the skin, pull up on the flesh as you go. Remove any
  bones with tweezers and cut into four equal-sized portions.
  Season each portion with salt, then roll the halibut in the
  lemon–herb mixture. Cover and refrigerate until ready to cook.

To prepare the SALSIFY, remove the peel from the Meyer lemons
  with a vegetable peeler. Reserve the peel and cut each lemon
  in half. Juice the lemons. Place the lemon juice and water in a
  large, noncorrosive container. Discard the lemons.

Peel the salsify one stalk at a time, then immediately immerse in
  the acidulated water. Salsify tends to oxidize (turn brown) very
  quickly if not in contact with acid or cooked at once. Once
  peeled, working with one stalk at a time, cut in ¼-inch rounds,
  returning to the acidulated water as you finish.

To make the herb sachet, lay a piece of cheese cloth flat on your
  work surface and bundle the reserved lemon peel, reserved
  herb stems, bay leaves, and peppercorns in the center. Pull up
  on all sides and tie with butcher's twine to create a sachet. Set
  aside.

About 30 minutes before serving, remove the fish from the
  refrigerator and allow to come to room temperature. Heat
  the olive oil and the herb sachet in a 10-inch stockpot over
  a low flame. Bring the oil to 150 degrees F (use a deep-fry
  thermometer).

Drain the salsify, pat dry, and add to the stockpot, cooking for about
  20 minutes, or until nearly tender.

MEYER LEMON–MINT RELISH
3 Meyer lemons
1 shallot
½ cup chopped briny
    green olives like
    cerignola or arbequina
2 tablespoons chopped
    fresh mint
Extra-virgin olive oil
Salt and cracked black pepper

While the salsify cooks, make the MEYER LEMON–MINT RELISH.

Cut the top and bottom off each Meyer lemon. Using a sharp knife, slice down between the pith and the flesh of the lemon, following the curve of the fruit. Repeat until all the peel and pith are removed. Cut between the membranes to release the flesh, making sure you work over a bowl to capture all the juice. Remove any seeds and set aside the segments.

Finely dice the shallot, move to a small bowl, and cover with the reserved lemon juice. Season with a few pinches of salt. This will macerate the shallots and remove some of the raw sulfurous properties. Let rest for a few minutes.

Roughly chop the reserved lemon segments, then combine with the shallot mixture, the olives, and the mint. Season with salt and pepper and pour in a bit of olive oil to taste. Set aside.

When the salsify is almost tender, add your fish to the stockpot. Lower the flame until the oil registers 140 degrees F. You should not see the oil bubbling but should be able to feel the fish firm up as it cooks. The halibut should be ready in about 8 to 10 minutes. Use a slotted spatula to lift the fish and check to see that it is opaque throughout.

When ready to serve, place a tablespoon or so of poaching oil in a small sauté pan and heat over medium high. Add the spinach and cook just until wilted; season to taste with salt. Divide the spinach between four plates. Using a slotted spatula, lift up one portion of the fish and one-quarter of the salsify and place on top of the spinach. Repeat with the remaining plates. Using a Microplane, grate some fresh Meyer lemon zest on top of the fish, then spoon relish around the fish.

SCALLOP TARTARE WITH AVOCADO–CITRUS SALAD AND FRIED GINGER

The bright, clear flavors of lime and orange sing in this Asian-toned first course by Chef James Walt of Araxi in Whistler, B.C. The firm, sweet flesh of impeccably fresh Pacific scallops needs no cooking, just a light "cure" from the citrus and salt with just a touch of heat. Maldon is a British sea salt harvested from the Blackwater River with a soft, flaky texture. **MAKES 4 SERVINGS**

12 medium fresh Pacific or
    weathervane scallops
3 tablespoons extra-virgin
    olive oil
Juice and zest of 1 lime
½ teaspoon pink peppercorns,
    crushed
1 small jalapeño pepper,
    seeded and minced
1 green onion, green part
    only, minced
8 cups vegetable or peanut oil
    (for deep-frying)
1-inch piece fresh ginger,
    peeled and cut as thinly
    as possible
1 large orange
1 teaspoon Maldon or sea salt
1 ripe avocado, thinly sliced
Handful micro greens
    or baby lettuces

Using a sharp knife, cut the scallops as thinly as possible to obtain four to five slices from each one. Place the scallops in a stainless-steel bowl, then add the olive oil, lime juice, lime zest, pink peppercorns, jalapeño pepper, and green onion. Toss gently to combine and refrigerate the mixture for 1 to 2 hours, or until well chilled.

While the scallops are chilling, fill a deep-sided skillet or wok two-thirds full with oil and heat it to 330 degrees F (use a deep-fat thermometer). Put the ginger in a colander and set it under cold running water for 10 minutes to soften the flavor. Pat the ginger dry with a tea towel. Deep-fry the ginger until crisp and golden, about 3 minutes, then remove from the oil and drain on paper towels.

Using a sharp knife, cut the top and bottom off the orange, then cut down the sides to remove all peel and pith. With a paring knife, cut out individual segments from the membrane, removing any seeds. Set aside.

When ready to serve, sprinkle the scallops with the Maldon and toss gently. Arrange a quarter of the avocado slices on each of four plates. Top with alternating layers of scallops and orange segments until you have three layers altogether. Spoon some of the scallop marinade over each serving and garnish with the micro greens and fried ginger.

Plum

(Prunus)

Many plum varieties love the Pacific maritime climate. They grace yards with quantities of showy pink or white blossoms in spring and follow the flower show with a multitude of juicy fruits, often in early summer when other fruits are still babies. They are hardy trees that need little attention and are known to bear prolific crops of good quality fruit. What more can you ask from a fruit tree?

A plum tree is relatively small and can easily be kept to a manageable size for harvesting. Even though some varieties are self-pollenizing, having another tree within fifty feet is a good idea. Be sure, when planting two trees, that they are varieties whose bloom times overlap. A late-blooming tree will be too late to help the bees pollinate that early bloomer. If you only have room in your yard for one tree, and there are no others in your neighbors' yards, go for a Santa Rosa, Italian, or Damson. These varieties are the best at self-pollenizing.

There are two main cultivated plum types—European and Japanese—and then some hybrids of these. The European plums are often blue hued and usually mature during late summer or early fall. Prunes are a kind of very sweet European plum. The extra sugar allows them to be dried in the sun without having to remove the pit. Japanese plums are the red, early-bearing types and what we usually see in the grocery stores. Several gardeners have reported having small, very tart plum trees in their yards that either sprouted on their own or were "just always there." Often these gardeners enjoy the blossoms in the early spring but leave the fruit for the birds. These are probably plums that are native to their area.

If you have late frosts, a European plum will probably be best for your yard. European varieties such as Green Gage like colder winters. Their fruit is usually smaller but has more sugar than the Japanese varieties. The blooms of the Japanese varieties, like Santa Rosa, can be damaged by frost and need less winter chill, so they are better suited for warmer, temperate climates. Plums have shallow roots and for that reason they don't like to have anything planted under them. Give them a little help by keeping the weeds away from the trunk of the tree and cut off any suckers (shoots) that sprout up from the base. Many vigorous plums will send up quite a few bright green watersprouts straight up out of lateral branches. Be sure to snap or cut these off as soon as you notice them.

When selecting a tree for your garden, keep the visual effect in mind: the Santa Rosa plum will grow into a traditional-shaped "lollipop" tree, while the improved French Prune is more upright, like a candelabra. A young prune tree will appreciate being staked for its first couple of years. Japanese plums can put out lots of new growth, so for the first three years they may need conscientious pruning to keep the shape and height you want. Some varieties like to grow upright, and you will want to cut the inside branches to spread them out

more. Other varieties tend to sprawl, so you will want to cut the outside branches. Aim for a vase shape for your tree. Older trees need little pruning after you have removed the watersprouts and the suckers and any dead branches, but prune to keep your tree from getting so tall you can't reach that perfect plum on the very top.

European plums branch with less gusto than the Japanese kinds do, and you can mostly let them grow as they will after the first few years and just prune back the new growth annually. Both the European and Japanese bear fruit on long-lived spurs, which are abundant and look like two- to three-inch pointy shoots covering the branches on Japanese plums and four- to six-inch shoots on European trees. Don't prune these, and don't worry that you will get these confused with watersprouts, which will grow much longer than six inches.

Although it may be hard to imagine that your plum tree could give you too much fruit, the Japanese plums might try. If so, it's good to take some them off the tree when they are very small, usually in early June. Break up clusters of fruit and leave four to six inches between fruits. Besides possibly breaking branches, leaving a too heavy crop to ripen could reduce your crop for the next year. European plums seldom need to be thinned, but if you do have an overabundant crop, thin them to three to four inches apart.

Plums are more pest free than many other fruit trees, but it is still a good idea to pick up all fallen fruit. In the cool maritime climate, a couple of gardeners mentioned that they had problems with the fungal disease known as black knot on their trees. It looks just like the name says. It is a knot on a branch of soft green tissue when it's young, turning black as it ages. This sounds like a dire disease indeed, but it is fairly easily controlled if you notice it before it spreads too far. Simply cut the branch at least three inches below the knot and burn the knotty branch or bury it deeply. If you are cutting more than one branch, be sure to use alcohol to clean your clippers after each cut so you don't reinfect the tree.

Blue jays and squirrels love plums! You will have to keep a close eye to compete with them as the fruit ripens. You can start tasting earlier in the season, but try to leave most of your plums on the tree until they are ripe or almost ripe. How can you tell? Look for the right color for your variety and give it a little squeeze. When they are just slightly soft, gently twist one off and sample it. The European plums should stay on the tree till good and ripe, but you can pick Japanese plums when they are a little underripe and store them in a cool, dry place or put them in a loosely closed paper bag to speed up the process. When they are fully ripe, these plums will stay good in the refrigerator for several days.

Best Bets for Plums

The following lists tell which plums are suited to their respective zones. There are likely many more varieties that would grow well in each zone; however, these are the ones that experts most highly recommend.

BEST BETS FOR ZONE 8B

BEAUTY. Similar to the Santa Rosa with a wonderful blend of rich flavors, this Japanese plum tree grows quickly and starts producing early. The bright red fruit is medium-sized and has amber-streaked flesh. Ripens in early August. Get ready to eat, because like all Japanese plums, they don't keep well. Partially self-fertile and bears better with another tree.

METHLEY. A cross between Japanese and European plum varieties, this tree needs little pruning, has great structure, and is loaded with thousands of sweet plums by July. All of the fruit ripens within about ten days, so have your basket ready. The fruit is reddish-purple and medium sized. The tree starts bearing when young and is a reliable, regular fruit producer. Self-fertile.

GREEN GAGE. A popular old English variety, this European plum bears large crops of not-so-pretty yellowish-green plums that have outstanding rich, sweet flavor. The oval fruit is juicy and firm yet tender. Good for baking, jams, and canning. An interesting thing about the Green Gage is that when it is cooked it changes its color from golden to pink with an orange tinge. Self-fertile.

SENECA. This European plum is a sweet, comparatively large freestone with beautiful reddish-purple skin and yellow or orange flesh. The plums grow vigorously on a tree that grows upright but doesn't get very big. Ripens in early September. Needs a pollenizer.

VICTORIA. A dark-pink, large, oval plum with golden-yellow sweet flesh, this European plum comes from trees that produce multitudes of freestone plums that are prized for canning and jam. This is England's most widely planted plum. Self-fertile.

BEST BETS FOR ZONE 8A

HOWARD MIRACLE. Its unexpected and delectable flavor is like grapefruit or melon or maybe pineapple! The fruit is large, crimson and yellow, and very juicy. The trees of this Japanese plum are vigorous and spreading. Needs another Japanese variety for pollination.

HOLLYWOOD. This is a beautiful ornamental tree that also provides abundant crops. It has dark-purple leaves and is loaded with showy pink blossoms early each spring. In August it produces large round, dark-red plums with deep-red flesh that are delicious when eaten fresh and make a pretty jelly. Grows to twelve feet tall and is disease resistant. Needs another Japanese variety for pollination.

OULLINS. A beautiful, pale golden-skinned Gage-type plum with dense greenish-yellow flesh, this European plum can produce well even in a wet spring. It is a sweet and tender fruit that is a little less juicy than many plums, which makes it well suited for freezing or canning. The tree is vigorous and, though it doesn't give you abundant crops, it is a regular and dependable producer. Self-fertile.

ITALIAN PLUM. An intensely sweet, small, dark purple, freestone plum with firm amber flesh that is great for eating fresh or for drying. Productive, reliable, and easy to grow, this European plum ripens in late August. Self-fertile.

BEST BETS FOR ZONE 9B

SHIRO. This classic hardy and reliable coastal Japanese plum can survive and be very productive even after a cold, wet spring. Round or egg-shaped, mildly flavored, bright-yellow fruit is great for fresh eating and for canning. Ripens in midspring. Best pollinated with another Japanese plum variety.

SANTA ROSA. This popular early-season Japanese variety has big purplish-red plums with aromatic sweet yellow flesh and tart skin. It is an old-time favorite for good reason. If you like that sweet–tart combination, there is no better way to get it than a Santa Rosa plum. Prolific and vigorous, self-fertile.

BEAUTY. Similar to Santa Rosa with a wonderful blend of rich flavors, this tree grows quickly and starts producing early. The bright-red fruit is medium sized and has amber-streaked flesh. This Japanese plum may be the best fruit in a mild winter climate. Ripens in early August—and get ready to eat, because like all Japanese plums, these Beauties don't keep. Partially self-fertile, so it is a good idea to plant another variety to ensure good crops.

ELMA'S SPECIAL. An heirloom European plum from Bellingham, Washington, this variety ripens early and has juicy, sweet fruit with amber flesh. The tree is reliable and bears at an early age. Self-fertile.

DAMSON. This dark-blue, late-season European plum tree bears small round fruits that have an intense sweet–tart flavor. Terrific for desserts and jam. When fully ripe, they are also great right off the tree. Self-fertile.

IMPROVED FRENCH PRUNE. This late-season European variety with small reddish-purple, very sweet fruit is classically dried but too sweet to can. It is unequaled for jam and other desserts and makes great fresh eating when fully ripe. The tree is productive and a regular bearer. Self-fertile.

ITALIAN PRUNE. This late-season European prune plum with dark-purple skin and amber flesh is terrific for fresh eating on the coast and better for drying in the hotter inland areas. Self-fertile.

BEST BETS FOR ZONE 9A

SANTA ROSA. This popular early-season Japanese variety bears big purplish-red plums with aromatic sweet yellow flesh and tart skin. It is an old-time favorite for good reason. If you like that sweet–tart combination, there is no better way to get it than a Santa Rosa plum. Prolific and vigorous, it is self-fertile.

MARIPOSA. Originating in Southern California, this large and egg shaped Japanese variety has glossy maroon skin and dark-red flesh. Delicious fresh or cooked, it is almost freestone and extremely juicy with excellent flavor. Needs a pollenizer.

SATSUMA. This Japanese variety produces heavy crops of large, dark-red plums with dark-red firm flesh in late July to early August. The pits are small, and the fruit is excellent for fresh eating, cooking, preserving, and wine making. Needs a pollenizer.

ELEPHANT HEART. Smooth, tart-tasting skin with ruby-red juicy flesh and excellent flavor and tropical overtones, this Japanese plum produces abundant yields and makes this variety a big favorite. Needs a pollenizer.

SUGAR PRUNE. A large European prune developed by Luther Burbank that is very sweet with reddish-purple skin and greenish-yellow fruit. Self-fertile.

ITALIAN PRUNE. This is another late-season European prune plum with dark-purple skin and amber flesh. Terrific for fresh eating on the coast and better for drying in the hotter inland areas. Self-fertile.

BEST BETS FOR ZONE 10

SANTA ROSA. This popular early-season Japanese variety has big purplish-red plums with aromatic sweet yellow flesh and tart skin. It is an old-time favorite for good reason. If you like that sweet–tart combination, there is no better way to get it than a Santa Rosa plum. Prolific and vigorous, self-fertile.

SATSUMA. This Japanese variety produces heavy crops of large, dark-red plums with dark-red firm flesh in late July to early August. The pits are small, and the fruit is excellent for fresh eating, cooking, preserving, and wine making. Needs a pollenizer.

BURGUNDY. This Japanese plum consistently scores high in taste tests. It is sweet with a mild, mellow flavor and little to no tartness. It has maroon skin with deep-red flesh. Unlike most plums, the fruit can ripen and stay on the tree for a month or so. Self-fertile and a good pollenizer for other plums.

MARIPOSA. Originating in Southern California, this Japanese variety is large and egg shaped with glossy maroon skin and dark-red flesh. Delicious fresh or cooked, it is almost freestone and extremely juicy with excellent flavor. Needs a pollenizer.

IMPROVED FRENCH PRUNE. This late-season European variety with small reddish-purple, very sweet fruit is classically dried but too sweet to can. It is unequaled for jam and other desserts and make great fresh eating when fully ripe. The tree is productive and a regular bearer. Self-fertile.

ITALIAN. Great for fresh eating and drying, this European prune is freestone with firm golden-yellow flesh and dark-purple skin. This productive variety ripens in August and is reliable and easy to grow. Best with another variety nearby for pollination.

GREEN GAGE. This popular old English variety bears large crops of not-so-pretty yellowish-green plums that have outstanding rich, sweet flavor. The oval fruit is juicy and firm yet tender. Good for baking, jams, and canning. An interesting thing about the Green Gage is that when it is cooked its color changes from golden to pink with an orange tinge. Self-fertile.

THE GLORIOUS PLUM HARVEST

Many backyard gardeners say that they eat most of their plums fresh and uncooked. This notwithstanding, the plum has multiple uses in the kitchen. Plums make great crisps or tortes. Have you ever tried mashed plum mixed into a muffin batter or baked plum halves mixed in with a rye bread? A plum pizza with cheese and nuts is a wonderful surprise and a soup of stewed and puréed plums with yogurt or sour cream and honey is a great lunch on a summer day.

MOROCCAN CHICKEN TAGINE WITH BROOKS PRUNES AND WALLA WALLA SWEETS

Café Velo chef-owner Rick Wilson developed this gorgeous tagine to highlight Brooks prunes, a variety grown in the Willamette Valley, just southwest of Portland, bred specifically to be dried. However, anyone with a prolific plum tree would be well served to invest in a dehydrator, extending your harvest and your delicious options for using your fruit. Though the ingredient list is long, the technique couldn't be simpler: Layer the vegetables and meat with the fruit and spices and let it do its thing.

You can certainly serve the tagine without the HARISSA OIL (recipe follows), but it adds a complex, fiery vibrancy that works beautifully with the sweet prunes and onions. It's quite addictive, really, and lovely on fish, chicken, garbanzos, even tossed with steamed carrots. This dish is especially delicious when served over couscous and garnished with Marcona almonds and fresh mint. MAKES 6 TO 8 SERVINGS

CHICKEN TAGINE

4 large sweet onions, preferably Walla Walla, halved and cut into thin slices

2 teaspoons ground turmeric

1 tablespoon ground cumin

2 teaspoons ground ginger

Place the onions in a single deep layer in a 4- to 6-quart cast iron Dutch oven or casserole. Sprinkle with the turmeric, cumin, ginger, black pepper, and saffron and toss briefly until coated. Use your index finger to distribute the prunes, poking them down into the onions. Arrange the chicken thighs on top in one tight layer. Dot with butter and add the water and cinnamon sticks. Set over high heat. Bring to a boil, then quickly reduce the heat to maintain a gentle simmer. Cover.

1 teaspoon coarsely ground
    black pepper
20 saffron threads, crumbled
8 ounces Brooks prunes,
    pitted
12 bone-in chicken thighs,
    skin removed
1 stick (½ cup) unsalted
    butter
3 cups water
2 cinnamon sticks
2 cups cooked chickpeas
    (if canned, rinsed and
    drained)

HARISSA OIL
1 cup extra-virgin olive oil
8 tablespoons ground paprika
2 tablespoons ground cumin
2 tablespoons ground
    coriander
1 teaspoon ground fennel seed
¼ teaspoon ground cayenne
    pepper
1 clove garlic, crushed
Sea salt

After 30 to 45 minutes, turn the chicken thighs over, making sure they are still fully immersed in the cooking liquid. Continue to cook for another hour or so. You'll know the chicken is done when it's tender and begins to fall off the bone. Stir in the chickpeas 5 to 10 minutes before serving and heat through. Season with sea salt to taste. Drizzle liberally with harissa oil (recipe follows) at the table.

To make the HARISSA OIL , stir together the olive oil, paprika, cumin, coriander, fennel seed, cayenne pepper, and garlic in a small bowl. Add sea salt to taste. Pour the mixture into a squeeze bottle and enjoy!

CORNMEAL RICOTTA CAKE WITH FRUIT

Think of this crunchy, not-too-sweet, altogether spectacular cake as a canvas. Pastry Chef Karra Wise of Seattle's Columbia City Bakery recommends sinking pitted cherries into the batter, garnishing the top with halved fresh figs or apricots before baking, or decorating the batter with concentric circles of sliced plum, maybe brushed with a little butter and sprinkled with sugar. In winter serve with poached or sautéed pears or apples, add a bit of chopped thyme or rosemary to the batter—you get the idea.
MAKES ONE 10-INCH CAKE

Recipe Note: This recipe makes a 10-inch cake in a fluted tart pan with a removable bottom. Wise thinks baking in individual tart pans is an exceptionally nice idea. If you do so, reduce the baking time to about 20 minutes total.

1 cup cornmeal

½ cup all-purpose flour

1 teaspoon baking powder

¼ teaspoon salt

1¼ cups ricotta

¼ cup water

½ cup plus 1 tablespoon honey

½ cup plus 1 tablespoon sugar

1 tablespoon grated lemon or
   orange zest

1 stick (½ cup) unsalted
   butter, melted and cooled

2 eggs

1½ cups sliced or halved fruit
   (your choice)

Preheat the oven to 350 degrees F. Oil a 10-inch fluted tart pan with removable bottom, or oil and put parchment in the bottom of individual tart pans or a regular 10-inch cake pan. In a small bowl, whisk together the cornmeal, flour, baking powder, and salt until combined. Set aside.

In a large bowl, whisk together the ricotta, water, and honey until smooth, or mix on low using a freestanding electric mixer. Add the sugar, zest, butter, and eggs, and mix until just combined. Stir in the dry ingredients and mix just to blend.

Pour the batter into the prepared tart pan and dot the top with fruit, sinking the fruit down as far as you'd like. You could also layer half of the fruit after adding half the batter, then place the remainder on top, and so on.

Bake for 35 to 40 minutes or until slightly golden and just firm to the touch (about 20 minutes for individual cakes). Let cool 5 to 10 minutes out of the oven, then use a sharp knife to release the cake from the pan. It will be slightly sticky and some batter may cling to the pan. Thankfully, after just one bite, no one will care.

PLUM SORBET

This intuitive and charming recipe for the perfect plum sorbet comes from San Francisco icon Judy Rodgers and The Zuni Cafe Cookbook, *a collection that lovingly inspires you to use all your senses when working with fresh produce. Rodgers chooses the Santa Rosa as her favorite plum for sorbet, but allow this recipe to guide you through using your own backyard treasures. Just make sure they are ripe and yield to gentle pressure.*

According to Rodgers, this is the one sorbet that is routinely better than the fruit you make it from. The purée accepts generous scoops of sugar, virtually guaranteeing a lovely creamy-chewy texture. With or without freckles of skin, this sorbet is intensely flavorful. If you have the opportunity, serve a few different types of plum sorbet together, showing off a few shades of pink, yellow, green, or burgundy and the complex, unexpected flavors of several varieties. **MAKES 1 TO 1¼ CUPS**

PLUM PURÉE
9 to 10 ounces ripe plums

PLUM SORBET
1 cup strained plum purée, with about 1 tablespoon reserved chopped skins
3 to 8 tablespoons sugar
Pinch of salt, if needed
Up to 1 tablespoon water, if needed
Up to 2 teaspoons grappa (optional)

Cut the flesh off the pits, working over a bowl so that you capture the juice. Purée or process, strain, and taste. Save some of the bits of skin you trap in the strainer. These flecks add a potent nose of acidity and flavor; so you may want to stir a spoonful back into the purée. This will make a beautifully flecked sorbet.

Taste the purée. Gradually add the sugar until quite sweet. See if a few grains of salt improve the flavor, then season the whole batch accordingly. If the purée is puckery or too intense, try adding a splash of water. In the event that it lacks dimension, a teaspoon or two of grappa can be ravishing. Try stirring a bit of the tart skin back into the sweetened purée, then add a bit more sugar to compensate.

Freeze a sample of the sorbet, taste, and correct as needed. Chill, then freeze according to the directions for your ice cream machine. If you have added the skins, they may collect on the dasher; scrape off and fold them back into the sorbet.

Fig

(Ficus carica)

When fresh figs are selling for five dollars a small basket in the stores, imagine picking these treasures by the handful in your own garden. A fig tree is an easygoing, just happy-to-be-here kind of tree. Easily grown, not much bothered by pests, it is pleased to be able to spread out in the ground or satisfied to be crowded into a pot. The tree itself is a thing of beauty. The huge, rich-green leaves contrast aesthetically with the gray bark.

Even in winter when the leaves have fallen, the silhouette of the tree is striking. Fig trees are long lived and, if you let them, can grow to more than fifty feet and spread even wider. The roots stretch out and grow far beyond the tree's canopy.

Figs are extroverted trees with huge exuberant leaves, which contrast with their complicated fruits with introverted flowers. The minuscule flowers are inside the fruit. The commonly grown figs, known as common figs, don't need pollenizers because they either have just female flowers or both male and female flowers inside the fig.

Even though figs are indigenous to hot, dry places, they can thrive in Pacific maritime climates. They are always best planted in a warm location with a southern exposure, or espaliered along the south side of a building. Choose your varieties carefully, especially if you live in the northern regions, as some varieties have better chances of giving you fruit than others.

Left to their own devices, figs shade out any plants trying to grow under them—clearly not a good choice for a small garden. But, wait—if you love figs, and who doesn't, there are ways to keep a fig both happy and productive and reasonably sized for your garden or even your patio. Your clippers will get a good workout. You can maintain a fig at a height less than ten feet tall and even less than five feet if you prune it, grow it as a bush, or plant it in a container. Many gardeners in the colder regions report that figs grown as bushes do better than those grown as trees. Growing a fig as a bush is a good way to keep it small enough to pick the fruit and give it more resilience if damaged by cold weather.

Training a tree to grow as a bush has two phases. The first phase is in early spring, just when you see a little bit of green appearing where the leaf will break out (known as bud break) and that is when you want to prune off any damaged or weak branches. On older bushes prune any unproductive branches to the ground. (You can mark unproductive branches the summer before with a twist tie or ribbon.) The second phase comes in midsummer, when you will pinch out the growing tips after the fourth or fifth leaf. This helps send out side shoots and prevents the tree from putting out fruit too early.

If you have the space to let your fig stretch out a little, you may still want to hold your tree to less than ten feet for easy harvest. When you first plant your tree as

PROPAGATE A FIG FROM A CUTTING

An unusual aspect of a fig tree is one of the most wondrous exceptions to modern fruit trees: it can be propagated from a cutting. One neighbor with a stunning and prolific tree grew hers from a two-foot cutting taken from her friend's ancient tree. If you want to try this, ask your neighbor or friend with a great tree if you can snip a few one- to two-foot branches from his or her tree in winter or early spring. Now you have a few choices. You can put these in water in a sunny window and wait till you see roots, put the cuttings in a bucket with potting soil, or simply stick them in the ground and cover them with mulch.

The advantage of the water method is that you can see the progress of the root production without disturbing the cutting or waiting till you see buds. Even though the leaves may fall off, don't give up because you may still get roots. After a couple of months put the ones with roots in pots for half a year, then transfer the best one to your garden. Not all of the cuttings will root, but even if just one does, you will have the start of a fig tree. That little snip of a branch will grow up to give you fruit in four to six years and could go on fruiting for another hundred years!

a bare root, cut it back by half. This can be hard to do, but it is all for the best as it allows the tree to focus on growing roots and side branches. At the end of the summer choose four to six branches that you want to produce fruit and prune away all the rest. At the end of the next harvest remove all the branches that are not growing out from your "fruiting" branches and take out any dead branches or suckers growing from the base of the tree. Also, take off any branches that are growing at less than a forty-five-degree angle from your fruiting branches. Finally, cut your fruiting branches back by a quarter or a third. Whew! This part is hard, like disciplining a sweet but headstrong child, but it will be better for all involved since more energy will go into making larger and sweeter fruit.

If you don't have room for even a fig bush, or if your winters just are too cold, try growing in a container. It is a little hard to believe that a vigorous, naturally huge tree could survive, let alone bear fruit, in a pot, but root containment may even help fruit production, although your crops will understandably be smaller than with a full-sized tree. Eventually, your fig tree will need a container that is fifteen to twenty gallons. Soil in pots will freeze faster than the open ground will. Roll your container into a garage or shed in the winter if your weather will be very cold, or wrap the pot with insulation.

In summer a black plastic pot could heat up so much that the roots could fry, and clay sometimes dries out quickly, so it's best to use a lighter-colored plastic, ceramic, or wooden container for your fig. Every three years in the spring (some people do this yearly), you will need to take the fig out of its container and prune the roots. Also, prune the branches down to six or seven feet to balance out the reduced root structure. Figs in containers do need some fertilizer annually, but go easy on the nitrogen so you don't just get leaf growth. You can lightly dig in some compost or use a water-soluble organic fertilizer with low nitrogen. (Look for numbers like "1-2-1" on the label. The first number is nitrogen.) If you have a huge yard and want to let your fig do as it pleases, simply prune for the first five years to get a strong scaffold for your tree, and then stand back and watch it grow.

It's easy to tell when a fig is ripe. The neck will bend and the fig will droop and soften. If you pick the fruit and see a milky sap ooze out, you'll know it is not at its optimum ripeness. That sap can be a skin irritant, so wash it off soon. For the sweetest fruit, wait until the figs are so soft that they all but fall into your hands. The birds like to test to see if a fig is ripe by taking a peck or two out of several of them. If you have a large tree, it's nice to share with the wildlife, but you may feel more protective of a small crop that you have pampered. To thwart their sampling, you can throw netting over a small tree. Don't forget to tuck in the netting at the bottom.

Many home garden fig trees bear two crops if it is warm enough. The first crop,

FIG

109

called the breba crop, bears on the previous year's wood and usually ripens in the spring or early summer. (If summers are cool, your fig may only bear a breba crop sometime in August.) A later, larger main crop develops and usually ripens in August or September, but don't worry if yours haven't ripened by then, as some gardeners tell us they don't get ripe figs until late October or even November. If it rains or you overwater and the ripe fruits split, be sure to pick these right away before the yellow jackets and other insects move in to feast on the sugary juice.

Water your new trees regularly until they are established. Some gardeners say they water their established fig trees in the summer, and others let them fend for themselves. The figs' origins are from the arid lands of the Middle East, so they are at least somewhat drought tolerant. Again, many gardeners rarely fertilize their in-ground figs unless they notice that the branches aren't putting out much growth, and others apply compost two or three times a year (but not too late in the growing season). Figs won't last long if sitting out on a counter, but they will keep up to a week in the refrigerator.

Best Bets for Figs

The following lists tell which figs are suited to their respective zones. There are likely more that would grow well in each zone; however, these fig varieties are the ones that experts most highly recommend.

BEST BETS FOR ZONE 8B

DESERT KING. This is a great choice for growing in the cool coastal maritime climate. This large, yellowish-green fig with strawberry-pink flesh bears one abundant breba crop in mid- to late summer on growth from the previous year. Prune carefully so you don't cut more than half of that growth. Self-fertile.

LATTARULA. This fig is one of the most popular varieties and has been reported to do very well in the coastal climates. It is a beautiful light greenish-yellow color when it is ripe. It can sometimes bear two crops in one season, one overwintering breba crop that will ripen in midsummer and sometimes another crop in mid to late September. Self-fertile.

BEST BETS FOR ZONE 8A

PETER'S HONEY. This variety ripens well in warm city climates or on the sunny side of a wall or fence and produces beautiful shiny, light-green fruit with delicious and tender dark-amber flesh. The late Peter Danna first brought this fig to Portland from his native Sicily. Self-fertile.

DESERT KING. A great choice for growing in the cool coastal maritime climate, this large, yellowish-green fig with strawberry-pink flesh bears one abundant crop in midsummer on growth from the previous year. Prune carefully so you don't cut more than half of that growth. Self-fertile

LATARULLA. This fig, also known as Italian Honey Fig, is one of the most popular varieties and has been reported to do very well in the coastal climates. It is a beautiful light greenish-yellow color when it is ripe. It can sometimes bear two crops in one season, one overwintering breba crop that will ripen in midsummer and sometimes another crop in mid to late September. Compact growth makes this variety a good choice for backyard gardening. Self-fertile.

NEGRONNE. This naturally small tree is well suited for containers or small spaces. The figs are a striking dark purplish-black color with rich, intensely flavored dark-red flesh. A delicious choice for the small garden. Self-fertile.

VERN'S BROWN TURKEY. There are many varieties of Brown Turkey, and many or most of those don't get on well with the maritime climate, but Vern's has proven itself here. It bears large, sweet, flavorful dark-brown figs with amber flesh. Often it will produce an overwintered breba crop and another crop in late summer. Self-fertile.

BEST BETS FOR ZONE 9B

DESERT KING. A great choice for growing in the cool coastal maritime climate because this tree doesn't like a lot of heat. This large, yellowish-green fig with strawberry-pink flesh bears one abundant crop in midsummer on growth from the previous year. Prune carefully so you don't cut more than half of that growth. Self-fertile.

LATTARULA. This compact tree, also known as Italian Honey fig, is one of the most popular varieties and has been reported to do very well in the coastal climates. It is a beautiful light greenish-yellow color when it is ripe. It can sometimes bear two crops in one season, one overwintering breba crop that will ripen in midsummer and sometimes another crop in mid to late September. Self-fertile.

NEGRONNE. This naturally small tree is well suited for containers or small spaces. The figs are a striking dark purplish-black color with rich, intensely flavored dark-red flesh. This is a delicious choice for the small garden. Self-fertile.

OSBORNE PROLIFIC. Also called Neveralla, this variety may be the best one for the maritime climate as the fruit ripens even in cool weather. The skin is reddish-brown with very sweet, pink-tinged amber flesh. This is another naturally dwarf tree that is good for containers. Ripens early. Self-fertile.

FIG

111

BEST BETS FOR ZONE 9A

BLACK MISSION. This teardrop-shaped fig has purple-black skin and strawberry-colored flesh with good quality and excellent flavor. The dependable and heavily bearing tree is long lived. It can bear two crops in a year. Self-fertile.

BLACK JACK. This naturally small tree is well suited to small spaces or containers. With large purplish-brown skin and amber flesh streaked with light red, this hardy fig has great flavor. It looks and grows just like a miniature Black Mission. Self-fertile.

BROWN TURKEY. This cold-hardy fig often bears two crops each year and is popular for fresh eating and canning. The medium-sized fruits are reddish to purplish-brown with reddish-pink flesh. It is a naturally small tree that does well in containers. Self-fertile.

KADOTA. This medium to large fruit has yellowish-green tough skin if grown inland and green skin if grown in the coastal areas. The flesh is red, juicy, and honey-sweet. This vigorous tree can bear two crops a year. Self-fertile.

PETER'S HONEY. This fig ripens well and produces beautiful shiny, light-green fruit with delicious and tender dark-amber flesh. The late Peter Danna first brought this fig to Portland from his native Sicily. Self-fertile.

BEST BETS FOR ZONE 10

BLACK MISSION. This teardrop-shaped fig has purple-black skin and strawberry-colored flesh with good quality and excellent flavor. The dependable and heavily bearing tree is long-lived. It can bear two crops in a year. Self-fertile.

BLACK JACK. This naturally small tree is well suited to small spaces or containers. With large purplish-brown skin and amber flesh streaked with light red, this hardy fig has great flavor. It looks and grows just like a miniature Black Mission. Self-fertile.

OSBORNE PROLIFIC. Also called Neveralla, this variety may be the best one for the maritime climate as the fruit ripens even in cool weather. The skin is reddish-brown with very sweet, pink-tinged amber flesh. This is another naturally dwarf tree that is good for containers. Ripens early. Self-fertile.

KADOTA. This medium to large fruit has yellowish-green tough skin if grown inland and green skin if grown in the coastal areas. The flesh is red, juicy, and honey-sweet. This vigorous tree can bear two crops a year. Self-fertile.

THE GLORIOUS FIG HARVEST

Many gardeners with fig trees say that they eat every single fig fresh off the branches and only give some away to their most special friends. Figs are delightful with a manchego or blue cheese. Warm them under a broiler and serve them with a salty prosciutto. Fig jam is delicious on almost anything, especially if it's made with a little Grand Marnier and lemon. If your small tree doesn't produce enough ripe figs at one time to make jam, it is perfectly fine, after washing and cutting off the stem, to toss the figs in a resealable plastic bag and put them in the freezer. You can continue doing this till you get enough for making jam.

GRILLED FIG AND GORGONZOLA BRUSCHETTA WITH THYME AND HONEY

Summertime, and the living is easy . . . especially with this beautiful first course from Seattle's Jerry Traunfeld, the perfect prelude to an evening spent on the patio. The kiss of heat softens the figs and caramelizes them just enough for beads of nectar to pool on the cut sides. The fresh thyme adds an herbal note while the Gorgonzola is just assertive enough to highlight the sweetness of the fruit and honey. As sophisticated as the flavors are, this dish is easy enough to prepare that you can enjoy yourself, too. MAKES 24 PIECES

    Recipe Note: Gorgonzola dolce is an Italian blue-style cheese that is mild in flavor with a creamy consistency that makes it easy to spread.

12 large ripe figs, halved
Few tablespoons extra-virgin olive oil
4 teaspoons chopped fresh thyme leaves 1 baguette cut into twenty-four ½-inch slices
6 ounces Gorgonzola dolce
3 tablespoons honey

Preheat a grill or broiler. Toss the figs with 1 tablespoon of the olive oil and 2 teaspoons of the thyme. Grill or broil the figs until heated through but not collapsed, about 1 or 2 minutes on each side.

Brush the baguette slices with olive oil, then grill or broil until toasted. Spread the Gorgonzola on the toasts and top each with a fig half. Drizzle with the honey and sprinkle with the remaining thyme. Serve warm.

FIG

113

GARGANELLI WITH BLACK MISSION FIGS, PANCETTA, AND LEMON

The honeyed sweetness of figs pairs perfectly with pancetta, rosemary, and a kiss of cream in this sublime pasta dish from Chef Lizzie Binder of San Francisco's Bar Bambino. Garganelli are hollow-ribbed cylinders resembling quill pen points. One of the key ingredients in the handmade pasta (recipe follows) is 00 flour, a very finely ground type used for pasta and pizza dough. In a pinch, substitute artisanal store-bought pasta instead. **MAKES 4 SERVINGS**

1½ cups diced pancetta

1½ cups diced yellow onion

2 teaspoons finely minced garlic

2 teaspoons finely chopped fresh rosemary

1 pound (½ recipe) hand-rolled garganelli pasta (recipe follows)

2 tablespoons butter

16 fully ripe Black Mission figs, stemmed and cut into coarse dice

Pinch of dried red pepper flakes

Pinch of freshly grated lemon zest

½ cup heavy cream

Freshly grated Parmigiano-Reggiano

Set a pot of salted water over high heat and bring to a boil. Meanwhile, in a heavy-bottomed pan, cook the pancetta until it is starting to turn lightly golden. Stir in the yellow onion and sweat in the pancetta fat until it is translucent and soft. Add the garlic and cook until the onion starts to turn a light golden brown. Remove from heat. Stir the rosemary into the warm mixture and set aside.

When the water comes to a boil, drop in the garganelli. Cook for 4 to 8 minutes, or until al dente (a little firm to the bite). While the pasta is cooking, brown the butter in a large saucepan on medium heat, taking care not to let it burn or darken too much. Stir in the figs and cook until they start to caramelize slightly. Add the onion–pancetta mixture, red pepper flakes, lemon zest, and heavy cream. Bring to a gentle simmer and cook until sauce thickens and becomes creamy. Taste and season with salt if necessary.

Mix in the cooked pasta and toss well to coat in the sauce. Serve immediately with a generous amount of freshly grated Parmigiano-Reggiano to finish it.

Recipe Note: You'll need a wooden dowel or a new pencil to form the distinctive quill shape, as well as a garganelli comb, a small grooved board, or even a sushi mat to create the ridges to hold the sauce. Chef Binder recommends Caputo or Ultra Performer brands of 00 flour, available in some specialty stores or online. MAKES APPROXIMATELY 2 POUNDS

GARGANELLI DOUGH

12 ounces 00 flour

12 ounces semolina flour

3 eggs, lightly beaten

1 tablespoon extra-virgin olive oil

1 to 2 teaspoons water

Begin by making a mound on your working surface of the 00 and semolina flours with a well in the center, like a volcano. To the well, add the eggs, extra-virgin olive oil, and 1 teaspoon of water. Incorporate by hand, until all the ingredients find their way into a dough ball. If the dough seems too dry, add remaining water.

Squeeze the dough on your surface with the heel of your hand, then shape it back into a ball. Continue this kneading for 15 minutes. Wrap the dough in plastic and allow to rest at room temperature for 1 hour.

Using a hand-crank pasta machine or an attachment to your electric mixer, roll out the pasta dough. Pass it bit by bit through the pasta machine, finishing on the next to thinnest setting. Cut the pasta sheets into 1½-inch squares. Place the pasta squares on the comb or sushi mat, with a corner of the square pointing toward you. Flour the dowel or pencil and position it so you can roll from one corner to the opposite corner. Roll to indent the pasta and seal the dough. Each finished piece will have two pointed tips and grooves in the dough.

Slip the garganelli from the dowel and arrange in a single layer on a towel, until ready to use in the recipe.

FIG

115

FIG MOSTARDA

Think of a mostarda (which translates as "mustard") as a spiced Italian chutney, a traditional accompaniment to boiled meats. Portland chef Cathy Whims of Nostrana says don't stop there. She recommends slathering it on sandwiches, serving alongside boiled or roasted meats, or adding a dollop to a cheese tray or platter of charcuterie. The combination of spicy mustard and honey-sweet fig is particularly lovely. For a Venetian variation, see the recipe in chapter 12, "Quince." MAKES 2 PINTS

3 pints figs, stemmed and roughly chopped

1 cup water

2 cups sugar

6 tablespoons dry mustard mixed with 3 tablespoons water

3 tablespoons black mustard seeds

Salt and freshly ground pepper

Place the figs in a heavy-bottomed saucepan over high heat. Add the water and sugar and bring to a boil. Reduce the heat to maintain a simmer and cook until the figs break down, about 10 minutes.

Stir in the dry mustard slurry and mustard seeds. Continue cooking until the sauce thickens and become thick and syrupy, about 15 to 20 minutes. Season with salt and pepper to taste. Cool and store in an airtight container in the refrigerator.

MARSALA-ROASTED FIG WITH ALMOND CUSTARD, VANILLA ICE CREAM, AND OAT TUILE

This gorgeous dessert from Pastry Chef Rhonda Viani of Vancouver's West Restaurant + Bar layers flavors and textures in such a way that you will rediscover the fig. This is a bit of an architectural dish, with the silky custard, the unctuous fruit, and the crisp tuile, all accented with a luscious homemade ice cream. To simplify things, use the best store-bought vanilla ice cream and offer a purchased cookie with some crunch as the counterpoint instead of making the tuiles.

If you do want to endeavor to make the charming oat tuiles, you can use purchased templates or make your own by cutting rounds out of thin plastic or even cardboard. You can also use an offset spatula to thinly spread rough circles of batter. Tuiles may be made up to two weeks in advance and stored in an airtight container until needed. **MAKES 6 SERVINGS**

ALMOND CUSTARD
⅔ cup ground almonds
½ cup confectioners' sugar
4 eggs
½ teaspoon vanilla extract
1 tablespoon flour
½ teaspoon salt
1 cup heavy cream
⅓ cup whole milk
½ stick (¼ cup) unsalted
   butter, melted

VANILLA ICE CREAM
8 egg yolks
1 cup sugar
1 cup whole milk
1 cup heavy cream
½ vanilla bean, split and
   scraped (pod reserved)

To make the ALMOND CUSTARD, line an 8-inch square cake pan with parchment paper and preheat the oven to 350 degrees F.

In a medium-sized bowl, whisk together the ground almonds, confectioners' sugar, eggs, vanilla extract, flour, salt, heavy cream, and milk until smooth. Add the warm butter. Pour the batter into the cake pan and bake for about 20 minutes, or until the top is lightly golden and a toothpick stuck into the center comes out clean. Allow to cool, then cut into 2-inch rounds. Set aside.

To make the VANILLA ICE CREAM, whisk together the egg yolks and sugar in a large heatproof mixing bowl, until the mixture turns a pale yellow. In a medium saucepan, bring the milk, heavy cream, and vanilla bean (both the seeds and the pod) to a boil. Slowly pour the hot milk mixture into the egg yolks while whisking vigorously.

Return this custard to the saucepan and cook on high heat, stirring constantly until the mixture coats the back of a spoon. Allow to cool, remove and discard the vanilla pod, then pour the custard into an ice cream maker and process according to the manufacturer's instructions.

FIG
117

OAT TUILES

1 stick (½ cup) unsalted
    butter

½ cup sugar

1 teaspoon vanilla extract

⅔ cup egg whites (from about
    5 eggs)

¾ cup ground oats

½ cup flour

½ teaspoon freshly ground
    cinnamon

MARSALA-ROASTED FIGS

6 large, ripe figs

4 tablespoons (¼ cup)
    unsalted butter

½ cup sugar

1 cup marsala

⅓ cup water

To prepare the OAT TUILES, preheat the oven to 350 degrees F and
    line a baking sheet with a silicone mat or parchment paper.

In the bowl of an electric mixer, cream together the butter and
    sugar until light and fluffy. Add the vanilla extract and egg
    whites and continue mixing, making sure to scrape down the
    sides of the bowl. Stir in the oats, flour, and cinnamon and mix
    until well incorporated.

Spread a thin layer of batter across a 2½-inch-round template onto
    the lined baking sheet. Remove the template, leaving a round
    disc of batter. Repeat until you have made six tuiles.

Bake until golden brown, about 8 minutes. Allow to cool. Tuiles may
    be made up to two weeks in advance and stored in an airtight
    container until needed.

To roast the FIGS, preheat the oven to 350 degrees F. Cut about a
    quarter off the tops of the figs and set the tops aside. Place the
    figs in a small roasting pan. Dot each fig with about 1 teaspoon
    of the butter. Sprinkle with sugar. Pour about two-thirds of the
    marsala over the figs. Place the reserved fig tops in the pan.

Roast in the oven until pink juices appear and the figs are heated
    through. Remove the figs from the pan and set aside. Deglaze
    the pan with the remaining third of the marsala and the water
    and pour the liquid into a small saucepan. Heat the marsala
    sauce on high until it is reduced to the consistency of honey,
    about 5 minutes. Remove from the heat and whisk in the
    remaining butter.

To serve, place an almond custard round in the center of each of six
    plates. Top with a fig, then drizzle with the marsala sauce. Place
    an oat tuile on the fig. Use a melon baller dipped in hot water to
    place a scoop of ice cream on top.

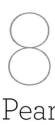

Pear

(Pyrus communis)

If you find yourself daydreaming about your garden and picture your future grandchildren picking fruit from a tree you fostered, plant a pear tree. These beautiful, prolific, and hardy trees can live and produce for more than a hundred years. Some people claim that instead of losing vigor, pear trees get even better over time. There are now two categories of pears on the block: the European pears and the Asian pears. They are similar in some ways but different enough to warrant some separate discussion.

In Europe, during the Middle Ages, pears grew as luxuries in castle and monastery gardens. The monks developed numerous new breeds so that by the Renaissance one grand duke grew 209 pear varieties on his lands. The pear came to the "new world" in the sixteenth century but was not as popular here as the apple because pears did not grow very well in the East Coast weather. Luckily for the pear, and for us, early settlers to the West Coast brought some pear varieties along with them, and pears have thrived in the Pacific maritime region ever since.

Pear trees are especially suited to these areas because, even though they prefer well-drained soil, they are generally more tolerant than other fruit trees of heavy clay soils. They require less chill time than apples and can produce fruit even in the notorious San Francisco fog, most notably Bartlett and Comice varieties, but in areas with the coolest summers pear trees will need a protected, warm area for the fruit to ripen well.

Pear trees are good candidates for espalier training. Without human intervention, they tend to grow upward more than outward, so they are well suited to the central leader shape but also do well trained in an open center shape. Head back upright branches annually to make them stronger and encourage lateral branching. Young Bartlett and Bosc pears are especially prone to their limbs breaking if the fruit set is too heavy, so if you see a weighty crop forming, a little thinning is in order. Do this when the fruit is small or let the fruit get a little larger and thin by picking off any blemished or misshapen fruit as you notice it.

If the variety of pear you decide to plant is self-fertile, it will still produce a better crop if it has another pollenizer tree nearby. If you have your heart set on Bartlett and Seckel pears, though, don't expect them to pass pollen back and forth, because they bloom at different times. The Bartlett may be the best at self-pollenization, so if you only have room for one tree, go for the Bartlett.

Typically, you grow fruit and wait and wait to pick it until it is ripe to perfection and only then pop it off the tree on its way to your mouth. This is not so easy where pears are concerned. A pear ripens from the inside out, so the pear that feels soft when you squeeze it is often overripe on the inside and may even be turning mushy around the seeds. Pears are best when they ripen to eating delicious-ness off the tree. If left on the tree, they won't develop the best flavor and the texture can be mealy or downright rotten in the middle. Knowing when your pear is ready to be taken off the tree may be something of an art that calls for observation and experimentation. Here are a few methods of assessing harvest readiness:

- Cup your hand under a pear, lift and twist your hand slightly. If the pear drops off into your hand, your timing is impeccable; if it doesn't fall with such little effort, leave it and check again in a day or two.
- A tricky way, at least until you get the hang of it, is to look closely at the small pores in the pear skin. When their color changes from white to brown, start picking.
- A grower of consistently delectable pears at a local farmers market has this rule of thumb: wait for one pear to fall and then pick all the rest of the fruit on that tree.

Now that you have a bunch of beautiful but not yet edible pears, find a cool place for them to ripen. Summer varieties will ripen pretty quickly while sitting on your kitchen counter, but if you store them below 40 degrees, down to 32 degrees Fahrenheit, you can keep them for several weeks and bring out a few at a time to ripen at room temperature. The flavor and texture of pears improve with their storage time off the trees. Cold storage slows the ripening so that the beneficial characteristics of the fruit can develop. Winter varieties, such as Comice and D'Anjou, like to be cold for about six weeks before ripening and will keep for two or three months. Winter Nelis and Seckel like to stay in a cool area, such as a basement; the Winter Nelis can be stored there all winter. If you are impatient for that first pear flavor burst, you can speed up the ripening process by putting a pear in a bag with a ripe apple.

Summer pears, like Bartlett, lighten in color as they ripen, but the winter pears don't always change color, so it can be harder to tell when these are ready to eat. Don't depend on squeezing. Gently press the area around the stem with your thumb. When it yields slightly, all the waiting has paid off and you can now enjoy your harvest.

Asian Pears

The explosion of sweetness along with the crunchy-crisp texture of the Asian pear might surprise you if you are expecting the soft flesh and buttery flavor of a European pear. Asian pears are round and not traditionally pear shaped, although some varieties have bigger bottoms than tops. They put on an impressive spring display of bright white flowers and will wow you with their gorgeous fall color. Many trees will turn a deep purplish-red and can be a beautiful focal point in your yard.

Asian pear varieties bear fruit when

the trees are young, sometimes at two or three years, and as they age they can bear quite heavy crops. Like most other fruit, this output could lead to small fruit every year or a large crop one year and a sparse or no crop the next, so you'll want to remove many of the newly forming fruit when they are young, leaving one fruit in each cluster. These trees grow vigorously on their own, so there is little need for fertilizer or much water, but they will need to be pruned a little more severely than European pears and can be easily espaliered. They are self-fertile, but as usual, your yield goes up if there is another Asian pear nearby.

Allow your Asian pears to ripen on the tree. They'll stay firm and juicy, and there is little guesswork involved to figure out when they're ripe. First check the color. Varieties that originally came from Japan will have yellow or yellow-brown skin, and the ones from China will have greenish-yellow skin. The skin will be thin and translucent

APPLES AND PEARS GROWING IN HARMONY

A fun project is to graft pear branches onto apple trees and eat pears from your apple tree. This will work best if you choose an apple variety that blooms at the same time as the pear variety. Imagine, apples and pears growing in harmony on the same tree!

GROWING PEARS IN A BOTTLE

One gardener was inspired to plant a pear tree just so she could try this! Start this project when the pears are very young (about one to two inches long) and use a beautiful, clean glass bottle. Long-necked types will give the most startling effect. You'll also need:

- wire or sturdy string
- clippers to snip branches
- green plastic grower's tape or more string

Wrap a piece of wire or strong string around the neck, just under the lip, and wrap the other end around the base, a couple of inches from the bottom. Slip the wire off the bottom and put the bottle aside. Because you will be giving this pear the royal treatment, you need a "king" pear, which simply means the biggest and strongest-looking pear in a cluster. If the king is at the end of a small branch, this next part will go easier. Search for a branch that hangs just below a sturdy higher branch. You will need this higher branch to hang the bottle on.

Snip off all the other little pears and leaves on the branch with the king pear. (Note: The bottle should tilt downward, so no water will get in and any condensation will run out.) Loop the wire or string a couple of times over the higher branch. Slip the wire back on the bottom of the bottle. Now carefully slide the small pear into the bottle almost all the way to the bottom. With the grower's tape or string, secure the wire at the neck of the bottle to the branch the pear is growing on, so that the bottle and the pear branch will move together in any breezes. Your work is done for now. Just stand back and watch the princely pear grow.

Your pear in the bottle is ready at the same time as the other fruit on the tree. Without bruising the pear, pull the branch out of the bottle as far as possible and snip it off about an inch from the pear. Do this while the bottle is on its side so the pear doesn't drop suddenly.

To get your pear clean, pour hot but not boiling water into the bottle and swirl gently. You might have to repeat this step more than once. When the pear is as clean as it can get, let it dry for about 20 minutes.

Fill the bottle almost halfway up the neck with spirits like vodka, brandy, or pear wine. Cork the bottle and display it on a shelf for all to admire for a couple of months until it's ready to serve to your lucky guests. If you have a long and very slender knife, the pear can be sliced and eaten.

looking. Now if you can get close enough, smell it to see if you notice a strong sweet smell. Lift one and twist it slightly. If the pear comes off easily in your hand, taste the fruit. If it's crispy and your mouth fills with flavor, you hit it just right. Not all of your pears will ripen at the same time, so remember how that perfect one looked and search for just the same thing again. Since the skin is so thin, place each one tenderly into your basket so it doesn't get bruised. Ripe fruit can be stored for ten to fourteen days at room temperature and three to five months in the refrigerator.

Best Bets for Pears

The following lists tell which pears are suited to their respective zones. There are likely more that would grow well in each zone; however, these pear varieties are the ones that experts most highly recommend.

BEST BETS FOR ZONE 8B

RESCUE. These huge pears are yellow with a bright reddish-orange blush and have a sweet, flavorful taste and smooth, juicy texture. The tree is vigorous and produces abundant, reliable crops even in the most coastal climate. Pears mature in September and keep until December. Good for canning and drying as well as fresh eating. Needs another European pear for pollination.

HARROW DELIGHT. This medium-sized flavorful pear from Ontario, Canada, is very resistant to fire blight and scab. It has a red blush over yellow with smooth-textured, nongritty flesh, making it a good dessert variety. It produces abundant fruit. Needs another European pear nearby for pollination.

BELLA DEGUINO. You will likely be the first to harvest a pear with this variety. It will be ready to pick in late June! The small-ish pears are red blushed, and the trees are sturdy and produce abundantly. Needs another European pear for pollination.

ORCAS. This vigorous, sprawling variety was discovered by horticulturalist and fruit explorer Joe Long in a hedgerow on Orcas Island in the San Juans and has become a regional favorite as it is so well suited to the maritime growing conditions. The yellow fruit with a carmine blush and buttery flesh is great for canning, drying, or eating out of hand. It is ready to pick in September. Needs another European pear for pollination.

BOSC. This is the pear most reached for by chefs because of its dense, almost crunchy flesh and sweet, slightly tart flavor. The fruit has a distinctive long neck and brownish-over-yellow russet skin. It produces abundant crops, and it's a great choice for a maritime region, but watch for any sign of fire blight in warm and moist weather. Needs a pollenizer.

The Asian pears that do well in this zone are the Shinseki, Chojuro, and Yoinashi.

SHINSEKI. Crisp and flavorful, with a slight taste of citrus, this pear has light-yellow skin and white crunchy flesh. The medium-sized fruit ripens in late August. It is partially self-fertile but produces a more reliable crop with another Asian pear as a pollenizer.

CHOJURO. People love this variety because of its distinctive aromatic, sweet flavor. The crispy large fruit has dark-golden russet skin. The abundant crops ripen in mid-September and keep until March. Best with a pollenizer, which can be another Asian pear or early-flowering European pear.

YOINASHI. Surprisingly, this fruit is said to taste like good butterscotch. The pears are large with russet orangey-brown skin and crisp, juicy sweet fruit borne on a vigorous tree that is resistant to pseudomonas. Needs a pollenizer.

BEST BETS FOR ZONE 8A

UBILEEN. This pear from Bulgaria is basket ready by late July or early August, and your baskets will be quite full of large, sweet aromatic pears because this tree bears an impressive crop. The flavorful fruit is fine textured and buttery. Needs another European pear for a pollenizer.

RESCUE. These huge pears are yellow with a bright reddish-orange blush and a sweet, flavorful taste and smooth juicy texture. The tree is vigorous and produces abundant, reliable crops. Pears mature in September and keep until December. Good for canning and drying as well as hot from the tree. Needs another European pear for pollination.

ORCAS. This sprawling variety was discovered by horticulturalist and fruit explorer Joe Long in a hedgerow on Orcas Island and has become a regional favorite as it is so well suited to the maritime growing conditions. The yellow fruit with a carmine blush and smooth buttery flesh is great for canning, drying, or eating out of hand. It is ready to pick in September. Needs another European pear for pollination.

The Asian varieties that do well in this zone are the Large Korean pear and the Raja pear.

LARGE KOREAN. This pear of many names is also called Korean Giant or Olympic or Dan Bae. These pears can be as large as grapefruit and weigh more than a pound each. The vigorous and winter-hardy tree starts producing at a young age. It blooms early in the season but doesn't ripen till early October. It is very sweet and crispy. The pears keep well, and you could be eating them all winter long. Needs another Asian pear for pollination.

RAJA. A new variety, Raja is a golden-brown, sweet, and richly flavored pear that grows on a productive, hardy, and disease-resistant tree. Needs another Asian pear for pollination.

BEST BETS FOR ZONE 9B

ORCAS. This vigorous, sprawling variety was discovered by horticulturalist and fruit explorer Joe Long in a hedgerow on Orcas Island and has become a regional favorite as it is so well suited to the maritime growing conditions. The yellow fruit with a carmine blush and smooth buttery flesh is great for canning, drying, or eating out of hand. A great variety for even the most coastal areas, it is ready to pick in September. Needs another European pear for pollination.

BARTLETT. This is the most popular pear in the United States and why not, with its richly sweet juicy taste and tender, smooth texture? The large pears turn yellow with a slight pink blush when fully ripe. A favorite for eating out of hand, baking, and canning. Needs another European variety for pollination.

BOSC. This is the pear that chefs reach for most because of its dense, almost crunchy flesh and sweet, slightly tart flavor. The fruit has a distinctive long neck and brownish-over-yellow russet skin. It produces abundant crops, and it's a great choice for

the milder parts of the coastal regions, but watch for any sign of fire blight in warm and moist weather. Needs a pollenizer.

COMICE. This large, yellow classic dessert variety with aromatic juicy flesh can be kept in the refrigerator and brought out to ripen through much of the winter, or stored for a month at room temperature to bring out the best flavor. Usually ready to harvest in early October, the Comice is fire-blight resistant. More fruitful with another European pear to pollinate it.

CONFERENCE. Hugely popular in Europe, this variety is sweet, juicy, and buttery with a pleasant flavor. Very productive, the large yellow pears hang from the branches like clusters of fat bananas. Ready for harvesting in October and November, it is great for eating and winter storage till January or later. This tree thrives in the maritime climate and needs another European variety for pollination.

The Asian pears that do well in this zone are the Chojuro, Twentieth Century, and Hosui.

CHOJURO. People love this variety because of its distinctive aromatic, sweet flavor. The crispy large fruit has dark-golden russet skin. The abundant crops ripen in mid-September and keep until March. Thin fruit heavily for good fruit quality. Best with a pollenizer, which can be another Asian pear or an early-flowering European pear.

TWENTIETH CENTURY. This crispy, sweet apple-like pear with yellow-gold skin grows on a small heavily bearing tree. Great flavor and keeps for up to six months. Self-fertile but is happier with a Bartlett or other Asian pear to pollenize.

HOSUI. This relatively new variety with mild, sweet flavor has a brandy aroma. The round pear has golden-brown skin with white speckles and juicy white flesh that doesn't keep as long as some of the other Asian pears—about four to six weeks in the refrigerator. It needs another Asian pear or a Bartlett for pollination.

BEST BETS FOR ZONE 9A

BARTLETT. This is the most popular pear in the United States and why not, with its richly sweet juicy taste and tender, smooth texture? The large pears turn yellow with a slight pink blush when fully ripe. A favorite for eating out of hand, baking, and canning. Needs another European variety for pollination.

D'ANJOU. A large pear with white, juicy flesh with a sweet flavor, it is light green with a yellow tinge. D'Anjou keep exceptionally well. Their best flavor comes out after one to two months of storage. The hardy tree bears abundantly and requires a pollenizer.

BOSC. This is the pear that chefs reach for most because of its dense, almost crunchy flesh and sweet, slightly tart flavor. The fruit has a distinctive long neck and brownish-over-yellow russet skin. It produces abundant crops, and it's a great choice for the milder parts of the coastal regions, but watch for any sign of fire blight in warm and moist weather. Needs a pollenizer.

SECKEL. This diminutive but famously sweet variety is also known as the sugar pear. The skin is russet yellow and the flavor is

---

MAKING PERRY (HARD PEAR CIDER)

Hendre Huffcapp is a great cider-making pear because of its balance of tannin and acidity. Making perry, or hard pear cider, is similar to making hard apple cider (see the sidebar "Hard Apple Cider" in chapter 4, "Apple"). The key to making really great-tasting perry is to start with good cider pears. Don't judge a perry pear by how it tastes fresh. It's breeding is for cider, not for out-of-hand eating. It is important to use pears that are ripe enough for the taste to be developed but not so ripe as to be mushy inside. For the best-tasting perry, let the crushed pears stand in a cool place overnight to lose some of the tannins and to help develop flavors before pressing in a cider press to extract the juice.

exceptional. It ripens in late September. It is fire-blight resistant and needs a pollenizer.

The Asian pears that do well in this zone are the Twentieth Century, Hosui, Shinseki, and Kikisui.

TWENTIETH CENTURY. This crispy, sweet apple-like pear with yellow-gold skin grows on a small heavily bearing tree. Great flavor and keeps for up to six months. Self-fertile but is happier with a Bartlett or other Asian pear to pollenize.

HOSUI. This relatively new variety with mild, sweet flavor has a brandy aroma. The round pear has golden-brown skin with white speckles and juicy white flesh that doesn't keep as long as some of the other Asian pears—about four to six weeks in the refrigerator. It needs another Asian pear or a Bartlett for pollination.

SHINSEKI. Crisp and flavorful, with a slight taste of citrus, it has light-yellow skin and crunchy white flesh in a medium-sized fruit that ripens in late August. It is partially self-fertile but produces a more reliable crop with another Asian pear as a pollenizer.

KIKISUI. This delicious, round, sweet-tart juicy fruit has tender skin that is yellow on a green background. The tree blooms late but produces an abundant crop. Best with another Asian pear for a pollenizer.

BEST BETS FOR ZONE 10

BARTLETT. This is the most popular pear in the United States and why not, with its richly sweet juicy taste and tender, smooth texture? The large pears turn yellow with a slight pink blush when fully ripe. A favorite for eating out of hand, baking, and canning. Needs another European variety for pollination.

COMICE. This large, yellow classic dessert variety with aromatic juicy flesh can be kept in the refrigerator and brought out to ripen through much of the winter or stored for a month at room temperature to bring out the best flavor. Usually ready to harvest in early October, the Comice is fire-blight resistant. More fruitful with another European pear to pollinate it.

SECKEL. This diminutive but famously sweet variety is also known as the sugar pear. The skin is russet yellow, and the flavor is exceptional. It ripens in late September. It is fire-blight resistant and needs a pollenizer.

WINTER NELIS. From Belgium the Winter Nelis is slightly yellowish-green with reddish-brown overtones. The small fruit is firm but buttery, juicy, spicy-sweet, and excellent for eating out of hand or baking. Can be self-fertile but sets more fruit with another variety as a pollenizer.

The Asian pears that do well in this zone are the Twentieth Century and the Shinseki.

TWENTIETH CENTURY. This crispy, sweet apple-like pear with yellow-gold skin grows on a small heavily bearing tree. Great flavor and keeps for up to six months. Self-fertile but is happier with a Bartlett or other Asian pear to pollenize it.

SHINSEKI. Crisp and flavorful, with a slight taste of citrus, it has light-yellow skin and crunchy white flesh in a medium-sized fruit that ripens in late August. It is partially self-fertile but produces a more reliable crop with another Asian pear as a pollenizer.

THE GLORIOUS PEAR HARVEST

Have you ever tried a green salad with cubed pears, Gorgonzola, and candied walnuts? It is terrific on a hot summer's day, and to warm you on that winter evening, you can't beat pear and butternut squash soup. Easy-to-make pear butter spread on your morning muffin is a terrific way to start a day, and a baked pear with a little cinnamon and brown sugar is the perfect way to end it.

GOLDEN PEAR SOUP

This healthy creation from vegetarian icon and Bay Area cookbook author Mollie Katzen combines fresh pears and sweet potatoes, puréed together and finished off with touches of cinnamon, white wine, and cream. This unusual soup is slightly sweet, slightly tart, and deeply soothing. It is easy to make, and it's hard to believe something that tastes this good can be so easy. This recipe is adapted from Katzen's classic Still Life with Menu. *The basic purée can be made ahead of time and refrigerated for a day or two before the finishing touches are added.* MAKES 6 SERVINGS

1½ pounds sweet potatoes, peeled and cut into small pieces (acorn or butternut squash may be substituted)

4 cups water

One 3-inch cinnamon stick

1½ teaspoons salt

3 large ripe pears (any kind but Bosc), peeled, cored, and cut into thin slices

1 to 2 tablespoons butter

¼ cup plus 2 tablespoons dry white wine

⅓ cup half-and-half, light cream, or milk (low-fat or soy is okay)

Few dashes of freshly ground white pepper

Place the sweet potatoes in a large saucepan with the water, cinnamon stick, and salt. Bring to a boil, cover, and simmer until tender, about 15 minutes. Remove the cover and let it simmer an additional 5 minutes over medium heat. Remove and discard the cinnamon stick. Set aside.

In a heavy skillet, cook and stir the pears in butter for about 5 minutes over medium heat, stirring frequently. Add ¼ cup of the dry white wine, cover, and simmer about 10 minutes longer over medium heat.

Using a food processor with the steel blade or a blender, purée the reserved sweet potatoes in the cooking water together with the pears-au-jus until smooth. (You may have to do this in several batches.) Transfer to a heavy soup pot or Dutch oven.

Stir in the half-and-half and the remaining white wine. Sprinkle in the white pepper. Heat very gently just before serving. (Don't let it boil.)

CHICORIES WITH PEAR BUTTER VINAIGRETTE, BRIE, AND CANDIED PECANS

Really a recipe within a recipe, this dish, created by Portland chef and Chez Panisse alum Troy MacLarty, begins with an unctuous pear butter. The butter is then used to sublime effect in a perfectly balanced vinaigrette that tames the bite of mixed chicories. Any greens in this family will do, such as radicchio, sugarloaf, treviso, castelfranco . . . use your imagination and what's in your garden or available at the farmers market. Candied pecans add crunch and Brie a lush richness. What a lovely way to eat your fruits and vegetables! As an added bonus you'll have pear butter left over to spread on toast, dollop on your hot cereal, or simply eat with a spoon. **MAKES 4 SERVINGS**

**3 heads mixed chicories,
    rinsed, dried, and
    roughly torn**
**¼ cup pear butter vinaigrette
    (recipe follows)**
**½ cup candied pecans
    (recipe follows)**
**½ cup Brie, cut into small
    cubes, room temperature**
Salt and pepper

CANDIED PECANS
2 egg whites
2 tablespoons water
**¼ cup sugar, plus 2
    tablespoons for tossing**
Pinch of cayenne
1 tablespoon salt
1 cup pecan halves

For the CANDIED PECANS, preheat the oven to 300 degrees F. In a glass bowl, lightly whip the egg whites, water, ¼ cup sugar, cayenne, and salt. Toss the pecan halves into this mixture to coat, then using a spatula, spread onto a baking sheet. Bake until the nuts are lightly browned and fragrant, stirring often to ensure that they are evenly coated. Remove the pecans and, while warm, toss with remaining sugar. The nuts will become crunchy as they cool.

To make the PEAR BUTTER, mix the pears, sugar, and cinnamon in a heavy-bottomed pot and cook over very low heat until the pears give off their juices and the mixture is reduced by half. Purée this mixture in a food processor until smooth, then return to the pot. Cook again over very low heat, until the mixture is fairly thick, stirring often to prevent scorching.

For the VINAIGRETTE, in a small saucepan, whisk the butter over medium heat until it is lightly brown and fragrant (it should smell nutty). Immediately transfer the butter to a small bowl and whisk in the olive oil to stop the cooking.

In another bowl, mix together the red wine vinegar, Dijon mustard, garlic, and the salt and pepper. Allow this mixture to sit 15

PEAR BUTTER

2 cups pears, peeled, cored,
  and roughly chopped

½ cup sugar

Pinch of freshly ground
  cinnamon

PEAR BUTTER VINAIGRETTE

3 tablespoons butter

¼ cup olive oil

2 tablespoons red wine
  vinegar

1 teaspoon Dijon mustard

1 small clove garlic,
  pounded into a paste

Pinch of salt and pepper

1 tablespoon prepared
  pear butter

minutes, then whisk in the olive oil–butter mixture and pear butter. Balance the flavors with additional vinegar, and the salt and pepper as needed.

Taste the pear butter vinaigrette for seasoning; it should be fairly assertive to balance the chicories. The vinaigrette should be slightly warm and creamy and drizzle-able. If it's too cold, warm the vinaigrette slightly over very warm water, whisking until you reach the right consistency. In a large bowl, toss together the mixed chicories with the vinaigrette, candied pecans, Brie, and salt and pepper to taste.

SHERRY-POACHED PEARS WITH A PEAR AND RAISIN COMPOTE AND MAPLE-ROASTED WALNUTS

When faced with a prodigious bounty of pears from your flourishing backyard tree, this recipe is the ticket—using the fruit in two glorious ways. Silken poached pears perch atop a honey-sweetened pear-raisin compote, a touch of black pepper adding the perfect bite. At Vancouver's West Restaurant + Bar, Pastry Chef Rhonda Viani nests the pear in toasted phyllo nests and uses a ring mold to give the appearance of a "whole" pear resting on the plate. If you'd like to follow her method, a biscuit cutter or can with the top and bottom removed will work for a ring mold. Of course, you may simply perch the poached pear atop the compote if you like, though the phyllo is easy to do and adds a lovely crunch.

MAKES 4 SERVINGS

4 ripe Bartlett pears,
   peeled and cored
1¼ cups oloroso sherry
⅓ cup sugar
Zest of ½ orange
¼ teaspoon ground
   black pepper
¼ cup raisins
2 tablespoons honey
Juice of half a lemon
¾ cup walnuts
¼ cup pure maple syrup

CRISPY PHYLLO
1 teaspoon honey
1 tablespoon unsalted butter,
   melted
2 sheets phyllo dough

Using a sharp knife, cut off the bottom half of each pear horizontally. Dice the bottom halves and set aside. Place the pear tops in a medium-sized saucepan with the oloroso sherry, sugar, and orange zest and simmer until tender, about 1 hour. Allow to cool. Remove the pear tops from the liquid and set aside. Heat ¾ cup of the poaching liquid on medium heat and cook for another 15 minutes, or until it reduces to a syrup.

Preheat the oven to 350 degrees F. In a small roasting pan, combine the diced bottom halves of the pears with the black pepper, raisins, 2 tablespoons of the honey, and lemon juice. Roast this mixture in the oven, stirring periodically, until the pears are tender but not mushy, about 30 minutes. Remove from the oven and allow to cool.

While the compote is roasting, spread the walnuts on a baking sheet and lightly toast them in the oven (at 350 degrees F) for 10 minutes. Shake them off and discard the skin from the nuts. Drizzle the walnuts with maple syrup and toss to coat. Return to the oven and, stirring every 5 minutes, bake until all the maple syrup has crystallized, about 20 minutes.

To make the CRISPY PHYLLO, lower the oven temperature to 325 degrees F and line a baking sheet with parchment paper. Whisk together the remaining teaspoon of honey and the butter and brush onto one sheet of phyllo dough. Place the other sheet on top and flatten with a rolling pin. Brush the top with the honey–butter mixture. Cut the dough into dime-thick strips and lay them out on the baking sheet. Bake for about 10 minutes, or until golden brown.

To serve, roughly chop the candied walnuts and toss with the pear and raisin compote. Divide the pear and walnut mixture among four ring molds the same diameter as the pear tops, pressing down gently with the back of a spoon. Carefully remove the rings. Place the poached pear on top and drizzle the poaching liquid syrup over the pear. Sprinkle phyllo strips around the pear to look like a nest. Voilà!

9

Persimmon

(Diospyros)

One of the most ornamental of the edible fruit trees, persimmons are stunning in autumn, when the large green leaves turn scarlet-orange and yellow, then drop to leave the fruit hanging like lit lanterns against the gray bark scaffolding of the branches. People grow persimmon trees for shade, as they can reach thirty feet and provide a beautiful canopy. However, they can also be kept to eight to ten feet with careful pruning. Most of the persimmons that are widely grown are Asian varieties.

One type is extremely astringent until it is squishy ripe because of the soluble tannins in the fruit. The other type is nonastringent. There is also a hardy native American persimmon that is rarely seen in stores but can grow in almost all forest habitats across the country; this type bears small astringent fruits that are quite tasty when left to ripen thoroughly on the tree.

The astringent Hachiya is shaped like a big acorn. Be ready for a mouth-puckering experience if you eat one before it is very, very soft. When fully ripe in the late fall, it loses the astringency and gets velvety and sweet like pudding. Strangely, mushy fruit is what you are looking for. The Hachiya can be frozen whole and then eaten out of its skin with a spoon, tasting not unlike a sherbet. The nonastringent Fuyu is about the size of a flattened baseball. It tends to ripen in the early fall, and you can eat the fruit like an apple, peeled or unpeeled, from the time it is very firm and crisp all the way until it is soft. The Fuyus can be kept on the counter for months and maintain their sweet and tart qualities. They can also be dried for a sugary treat to be enjoyed all winter long. While you are waiting to eat either kind of persimmon, pile them in bowls or line them up on the counter so you can admire their decorative color and shape.

Besides being beautiful, persimmon trees are easy and relatively carefree to grow because they have few problems with pests or disease and adapt well to all kinds of soils. Because they don't need much winter chill, they like our maritime conditions with our moderate winters and mild summers, but if there is a warm spell in the late winter or early spring that triggers them to break dormancy and start to put out buds, they could be damaged if another frost comes along.

Especially when the tree is young, you may have to do some searching to find the camouflaged blooms. The small whitish flowers are surrounded by a cuplike calyx (the group of four leaf-colored sepals behind the petals), which is much bigger than the flower and covers it like an umbrella. You may have more luck spotting the flowers if you lie on the ground and gaze up.

Patience is needed in more than looking for flowers or waiting for your persimmon to get ripe. Persimmon tree growers often lament how many years it takes for the tree to produce fruit. Up to six years is not uncommon, but it will go on to bear fruit for many decades. Many people advise against fertilizing persimmons because too much nitrogen can cause fruit drop. Even if you haven't fed your tree, dropping of immature fruit from May to September is not uncommon. This will be especially bothersome with a young tree, but once your tree is established, you will have plenty of fruit left even after some drop.

If you are going to let your persimmon grow to its intended height and breadth, there is little need to prune, but many backyard growers like to keep their trees short enough so that they can reach all the fruit without a ladder. To keep it small, start training your tree early by cutting it back to half its height, but not to less than three feet, before planting. Persimmon trees are often grown with a central leader, or main trunk, with a strong framework of smaller branches. Fruit grows in the axils—the points where leaf and branch meet—near the tips of one-year-old branches. Prune to thin branches closer together than six inches, to open up the center to light and air, and to remove any branches that are crossing into the center of the tree. Persimmons have a deep taproot, which makes them poor candidates for container growing, but they can be espaliered or trained to be a hedge.

The persimmon is a fruit without a hard-and-fast rule about when it should come off the tree, but you will undoubtedly want to take your persimmons down before they fall off on their own. Neither the Fuyu nor the Hachiya type will fall until they are squishy, and unless you are right there with hands open to catch that jelly-like persimmon, it will splat into a sodden mess on the ground. Also, the longer it is hanging ripe on the tree, the more time the birds, squirrels, or deer will have to beat you to your long-awaited gems. The signal to start thinking about harvesting is when the color of the persimmon turns from green to golden-orange. By the time it turns bright orange, the birds and other wildlife may have already started sampling. When the time is right, don't try to pluck or twist the fruit from the tree. Instead, get out your clippers and snip the branch close to the persimmon just above the calyx, leaving the pretty four-pointed "star" attached.

Both the Fuyu types and the Hachiya types can ripen on the counter, or you can put them in a paper bag with an apple for a day or two to speed the ripening. To extend persimmon season, unripe Hachiyas can be stored for up to a month in the refrigerator before being taken out to ripen on your counter. Both types can be kept fresh in the refrigerator after they ripen, and both are also delicious dried. The Fuyu type can be sliced and dried in a dehydrator or just-warm oven till dry and crisp and stored in an airtight container. Put a Hachiya in the freezer for a few days when it starts to soften. When you take it out, it will be soft and you can eat it like pudding.

Best Bets for Persimmon

The following lists tell which persimmons are suited to their respective zones. There are likely more that would grow well in each zone; however, these varieties are the ones that experts most highly recommend.

BEST BETS FOR ZONE 8B

SAIJO. Growing persimmon trees that will produce fruit in the cool summers of this zone is difficult, but if you have a sheltered area with lots of sun, try a Saijo. It produces consistently honey-sweet acorn-shaped fruit on a naturally small tree. This is an astringent variety, so don't even taste it until it is very soft. It is hardy to -10 degrees Fahrenheit, and it is self-fertile.

If you love, love, love persimmons and have that really warm microclimate in your yard, you could also try these nonastringent types:

ICHI KI KEI JIRO. This is an early variety of Jiro that produces large, flat-bottomed, deep-orange fruit that ripens in late October. Very cold hardy, and because of its naturally dwarf size, it is good for backyards. Self-fertile.

IZU. The Izu is also a relatively early-ripening persimmon with a cinnamon-sweet flavor. It sets medium-sized fruit on a dwarf tree. Very cold-hardy, self-fertile variety.

BEST BETS FOR ZONE 8A

The following astringent types of persimmons do well in this zone:

SAIJO. Growing persimmon trees that will produce fruit in the cool summers of this zone is difficult, but if you have a sheltered area with lots of sun, try a Saijo. It produces consistently honey-sweet acorn-shaped fruit on a naturally small tree. This is an astringent variety, so don't even taste it until it is very soft. It is hardy to -10 degrees Fahrenheit, and it is self-fertile.

NIKITA'S GIFT. From Ukraine this hybrid of Asian and American persimmons bears bountiful crops of exceptionally sweet and flavorful, two- to three-inch reddish-orange fruits on a tree that grows to ten to twelve feet. If possible, leave the fruit to ripen on the tree, which may not be until Christmas, after all of the gorgeous red leaves have fallen. What a beautiful gift to yourself! Self-fertile.

The following nonastringent types of persimmons do well in this zone:

FUYU. This is the most popular variety of nonastringent persimmons. The Fuyu is a heavy producer of crisp, sweet, mild-flavored fruit with a hint of cantaloupe. They do like long, hot summers. Self-fertile.

JIRO. This is the Fuyu-type persimmon most often found in the grocery store in the United States. The medium-sized bright-orange fruit with sweet mild flesh is one of the earliest Fuyu varieties to ripen. Self-fertile.

GIANT FUYU. Also known as Hana, the fruits are somewhat bigger than other Fuyu varieties and not as flat on the bottom. It has the reddish-orange skin of most Fuyus but with deep-red flesh when fully ripe. The tree is naturally small. Self-fertile.

NISHAMURA WASE. Sometimes called Coffee Cake because of its sweet, cinnamon pastry taste, this variety ripens a month before Fuyu, so it is an excellent choice for cool summer areas. The large, round fruit is sweet and rich tasting *only* when properly pollenized, so that seeds can develop. The best pollenizer is Chocolate (see description for Zone 9a).

BEST BETS FOR ZONE 9B

The following astringent types of persimmons do well in this zone:

HONAN RED. Dark orangey-red fruits are midsized and acorn shaped. They develop a smooth, fiber-free, very sweet, and richly flavored taste when fully ripe. Thin-skinned, heavy-producing trees. Self-fertile.

The following nonastringent types of persimmons do well in this zone:

IZU. A great choice for this coastal region, the Izu is a large and flavorful dark-orange fruit that ripens a month earlier than other Fuyu varieties and needs less heat. The productive, ornamental tree is naturally small. Self-fertile.

JIRO. This is the Fuyu-type persimmon most often found in the grocery store in the United States. The medium-sized bright-orange fruit with sweet mild flesh is one of the earliest Fuyu varieties to ripen. Self-fertile.

BEST BETS FOR ZONE 9A

The following astringent types of persimmons do well in this zone:

HACHIYA. This very large, cone-shaped fruit has bright-orange skin when ripe. It is considered to be the very best cooking persimmon. The fruit begins to ripen in October. The tree is upright, vigorous, and self-fertile.

CHOCOLATE. This complicated variety offers a spicy and complex taste treat when the seeds turn the pulp brown and soften the astringency. If no seeds occur, the fruit must get to the very soft state before the astringency disappears. This tree develops the best flavor when pollinated by another persimmon. The Nishamura Wase (also known as Coffee Cake) variety is the best pollenizer.

These nonastringent persimmons do well in this zone:

GIANT FUYU. Also known as Hana, the fruits are somewhat bigger than other Fuyu varieties and not as flat on the bottom. It has the reddish-orange skin of most Fuyus but with deep-red flesh when fully ripe. The tree is naturally small. Self-fertile.

JIRO. This is the Fuyu-type persimmon most often found in the grocery store in the United States. The medium-sized bright-orange fruit with sweet mild flesh is one of the earliest Fuyu varieties to ripen. Self-fertile.

NISHAMURA WASE. Sometimes called Coffee Cake because of its sweet, cinnamon pastry taste, this variety ripens a month before Fuyu, so it is an excellent choice for cool summer areas. The large, round fruit is sweet and rich tasting only when properly pollenized so that seeds can develop. The best pollenizer is Chocolate.

BEST BETS FOR ZONE 10

The following astringent types of persimmons do well in this zone:

HACHIYA. Very large and cone shaped, this fruit has bright-orange skin when ripe. It is considered to be the very best cooking persimmon. The fruit begins to ripen in October. The tree is upright, vigorous, and self-fertile.

CHOCOLATE. This complicated variety offers a spicy and complex taste treat when the seeds turn the pulp brown and soften the astringency. If no seeds occur, the fruit must get to the very soft state before the astringency disappears. This tree develops the best flavor when pollenized by another persimmon. The Nishamura Wase (also known as Coffee Cake) variety is the best pollenizer.

The following nonastringent varieties of persimmons do well in this zone:

JIRO. This is the Fuyu-type persimmon most often found in the grocery store in the United States. The medium-sized bright-orange fruit with sweet mild flesh is one of the earliest Fuyu varieties to ripen. Self-fertile.

GIANT FUYU. Also known as Hana, the fruits are somewhat bigger than other Fuyu varieties and not as flat on the bottom. It has the reddish-orange skin of most Fuyus but with deep-red flesh when fully ripe. The tree is naturally small. Self-fertile.

IZU. A great choice for this coastal region, the Izu is a large and flavorful dark-orange fruit that ripens a month earlier than other Fuyu varieties and needs less heat. The productive, ornamental tree is naturally small. Self-fertile.

MARU. This has brilliant orange-red skin with dark cinnamon-colored nonastringent flesh if it is pollinated and develops seeds. If it does not develop seeds, it will be astringent until it is very soft. The trees are vigorous and productive. Needs another tree, such as Chocolate, as a pollenizer.

THE GLORIOUS PERSIMMON HARVEST

Ripe Hachiya-type persimmons are used mostly for desserts and make wonderfully moist cakes and puddings with unique flavor. The tastes of Fuyu-type persimmons and ginger complement each other, and many recipes combine these ingredients. Tea made from fresh ginger and dried persimmons is an unusual treat, and doesn't bread pudding with soft Fuyus and raisins sprinkled with crystallized ginger sound comfortingly yummy? A curried soup adds curry flavors to persimmon and ginger. Mix Fuyu with onion, tomatillo, cilantro, and chiles for a great salsa. Or combine spinach with feta cheese and firm Fuyu with a simple oil and balsamic vinegar dressing for an inviting fall salad.

PERSIMMON AND FENNEL SALAD

This luscious winter salad is a favorite at Poppy, famed chef Jerry Traunfeld's Seattle restaurant. Chef Traunfeld uses a persimmon variety called Amagaki, sourced for the restaurant by their Japanese seafood purveyor, but any variety that is sweet when firm will work. Though it appears in a relatively small quantity, the coriander seed adds the perfect note to the dish. Please take the time to briefly toast the seeds, then crush with a mortar and pestle or spice grinder; the flavor will be so much more vibrant.
MAKES 2 SERVINGS, OR MORE AS PART OF A MULTI-TASTE MEAL

2 tablespoons fresh lime juice
1 tablespoon walnut oil
1 tablespoon clover or orange
   blossom honey
¼ teaspoon crushed toasted
   coriander seeds
¼ teaspoon salt
2 firm but ripe Amagaki or
   4 Fuyu persimmons, peeled,
   quartered, and sliced
Half of a fennel bulb, cut into
   very thin slices

Whisk together the lime juice, walnut oil, honey, coriander seeds, and salt in a mixing bowl. Stir in the persimmon and fennel, and toss to coat evenly. Serve right away.

GRILLED QUAIL SALAD WITH ITS EGG, CRISPED PANCETTA, WATERCRESS, AND PERSIMMON COMPOTE

While we may never know whether the chicken or the egg came first, in this recipe the quail and its egg appear in tandem to great effect. This fabulous dish from Chef Tom McNaughton of Flour + Water celebrates the glory of Fuyu-type persimmons, those squat beauties that are eaten when firm. The persimmon compote is delicious served on its own with other grilled meats or poultry (see chapter 12 for similar recipes for quince). If you're short on time, you can also grill the quail and just make the persimmon-watercress salad for an easier dish. However, you can marinate the quail up to forty-eight hours in advance to streamline preparation, and the compote is easily made ahead. MAKES 4 SERVINGS

Recipe Note: To ensure the pancetta crisps nicely, ask your butcher or the person at the meat counter to slice it very thinly for you. While you're there, ask pretty please would he or she debone the quail for you too? You can also look for deboned or partially deboned frozen quail at the supermarket if you can't find fresh. Quail eggs are available in most Asian markets and groceries.

3 tablespoons chopped fresh thyme

1 tablespoon olive oil

1½ tablespoons sweet wine, such as vin santo

4 quail, deboned and butterflied

Salt and cracked black pepper to taste

12 very thin slices of pancetta

⅓ cup apple cider vinegar

1 cup extra-virgin olive oil plus any leftover fat from cooking the pancetta

1 tablespoon whole grain mustard

1 tablespoon white vinegar

6 fresh quail eggs

4 ripe persimmons

Up to forty-eight hours in advance, in a glass dish, combine the thyme, olive oil, and vin santo and toss with butterflied quail. Season with salt and cracked black pepper. Cover and refrigerate until ready to use.

Preheat the oven to 350 degrees F. Place the pancetta slices in a single layer on a baking sheet. Nestle another baking sheet on top and put in oven. Bake the pancetta until crisp. Remove the crisps to paper towels to drain, reserving any accumulated fat.

To make the vinaigrette, in a small bowl, whisk together apple cider vinegar, extra-virgin olive oil, pancetta drippings, and mustard. Season with salt to taste. Set aside.

Set a medium pot to boil with water, white vinegar, and a handful of salt. Fill a small cup halfway with water. Gently crack the quail eggs into the cup. Fill another medium bowl with ice water. When the water has reached a boil, swirl the water with a wooden spoon and gently tip in the eggs and water from the cup. As soon as the eggs float to the surface, gently lift out with a slotted spoon and place in the bowl with ice water. The whole process should take no more than a minute to ensure the yolks stay runny.

2 bunches of watercress,
   rinsed and patted dry
Parmigiano-Reggiano (for
   shavings)
⅓ cup persimmon compote
   (recipe follows)

PERSIMMON COMPOTE
MAKES 2 CUPS
4 tablespoons (¼ cup) butter
5 Fuyu persimmons, peeled,
   cored, and cut into a fine
   dice
2 apples, peeled, cored,
   and cut into a fine dice
¼ teaspoon freshly
   ground cinnamon
¼ teaspoon freshly
   ground nutmeg
½ teaspoon freshly
   ground black pepper
3 tablespoons crisp
   white wine
1 teaspoon apple cider
   vinegar
1 tablespoon blanched
   yellow mustard seeds
1 teaspoon whole
   grain mustard

Heat the grill to high, but first oil a towel and rub down the grill to make sure the quail will not stick. Remove the quail from the refrigerator and allow to come to room temperature before grilling. Place quail breast side down first and grill for roughly 5 minutes. Turn and grill for another 5 minutes. The quail should be just firm to the touch; take care not to overcook. Remove the quail to a plate and allow to rest for at least 5 minutes before serving.

While the quail rests, place the quail eggs in hot water to gently reheat. Using a mandolin, shave the raw persimmons into a mixing bowl and fold in the watercress. Dress to taste with the vinaigrette, salt, and pepper.

To serve, place the persimmon-watercress salad on one side of a rectangle platter and place the still-warm quail and pancetta chips on top. With a vegetable peeler, make a couple of long shavings of Parmigiano-Reggiano to put on top of the warm salad. Nestle the poached eggs in the salad, being careful not to break them. Dollop the persimmon compote (recipe follows) on the opposite side of the plate and serve.

To make the PERSIMMON COMPOTE, melt the butter over high heat in a large sauté pan. Add the persimmons and apples and cook, stirring until the fruit starts to color. Mix in the cinnamon, nutmeg, black pepper, white wine, apple cider vinegar, and mustard seeds, then cover and reduce the heat to medium. Continue to cook for about 30 minutes, or until the fruit is tender and the mixture thickens. Stir occasionally and add a little water if necessary to keep the compote from drying out. When finished, season with the whole grain mustard.

ROASTED DUCK BREAST WITH CELERIAC, CHANTERELLES, AND PERSIMMON

Sweet, firm Fuyu persimmons and duck, edged in crisped skin, make for an inspired combination in this recipe from James Beard-nominated Seattle chef and restaurateur Ethan Stowell. Paired with two other Northwest fall favorites—celeriac, or celery root as it's more commonly called, and buttery chanterelles—this dish is a winner. Use any persimmon that is firm when ripe. **MAKES 4 SERVINGS**

4 ripe Fuyu persimmons
Four 5- to 6-ounce duck breasts, skin on
Olive oil
2 tablespoons butter
1 shallot, finely chopped
1 medium celeriac, peeled and diced
½ pound chanterelles, cleaned, ends trimmed, and cut into thick slices
Leaves from 2 sprigs thyme
3 tablespoons fresh parsley, chopped
Salt and pepper to taste

Preheat the oven to 375 degrees F. Slice the persimmons ⅛-inch thick using a mandolin or sharp knife. Using a biscuit cutter, cut circles out of each slice of persimmon to remove the skin. Divide the slices among four plates, overlapping slightly in a line. Reserve.

Film the bottom of a large, ovenproof sauté pan with olive oil and heat over medium-low for a few minutes. Season the duck breasts with salt and pepper, then add to the pan, skin side down, and cook for 8 to 10 minutes, or until most of the fat renders and the skin crisps. As the duck breasts sear, spoon off excess fat as it pools in the pan. When the fat has rendered, remove the duck breasts to a plate and pour off all the accumulated fat. Return the duck breasts, skin side up, and transfer the sauté pan to an oven. Roast for no more than 2 to 3 minutes, then remove from the pan and allow the breasts to rest while you complete the dish.

Heat the butter and shallot in a large sauté pan over medium-high heat. Cook until the shallot is soft but not colored. Stir in the celeriac and mushrooms. Season to taste with salt and pepper. Cook until the mushrooms have released their juices and the celery root is soft, about 3 to 4 minutes. Toss with the thyme and parsley. Be sure to check the seasoning.

To serve, divide the shallot–celeriac–mushroom mixture among the four plates, next to the reserved persimmon, and top with the duck breasts.

PERSIMMON PUDDING WITH PEAR BRANDY HARD SAUCE

This very special recipe for persimmon pudding first appeared in Seattle icon Tom Douglas's cookbook Tom's Big Dinners *and is the perfect vehicle for Hachiya-type fruit. Also called astringent persimmons, these become translucent when ripe and are only eaten when their flesh is as soft as custard. As individual persimmons ripen, Chef Douglas recommends popping them into a resealable plastic bag and tossing it in the freezer. Thaw your persimmons when you want to make this pudding.* MAKES ONE 9-INCH CAKE

Recipe Note: To make the persimmon purée, cut the persimmons in half, scrape out the soft flesh with a spoon, and purée the flesh until smooth in a food processor.

1½ cups persimmon purée (made from about 4 very ripe Hachiya persimmons; see recipe note)

3 tablespoons unsalted butter, melted, plus a little more for buttering the pan

2 cups buttermilk

3 large eggs

¾ cup firmly packed brown sugar

¼ cup granulated sugar

1 teaspoon pure vanilla extract

1 cup all-purpose flour

1 teaspoon baking powder

1 teaspoon baking soda

1 teaspoon freshly ground cinnamon

½ teaspoon freshly ground allspice

¼ teaspoon freshly grated nutmeg

Pinch of salt

Pear brandy hard sauce, room temperature (recipe follows)

Preheat the oven to 350 degrees F. Butter a 9-inch cake pan and line it with a circle of buttered parchment paper. .

In a large bowl, using a whisk, combine the persimmon purée, butter, buttermilk, eggs, brown sugar, granulated sugar, and vanilla extract. Whisk until smooth. In another bowl, mix together the flour, baking powder, baking soda, cinnamon, allspice, nutmeg, and salt. Add the dry ingredients to the wet ingredients and mix until just combined.

Scrape the batter into the prepared cake pan. Bake until a skewer inserted in the center of the cake comes out clean, about 50 to 60 minutes. Remove from the oven and cool 10 minutes on a rack. The pudding will sink as it cools.

To unmold the cake, run a thin knife around the cake to loosen it. The top surface of the pudding may be sticky when it is hot, so place a piece of lightly buttered wax paper over the cake pan, then cover with an inverted plate or a cardboard circle. Protecting your hands with a kitchen towel, invert the whole thing. The pudding should slide out onto the wax-paper-lined plate. Peel off the circle of parchment, then place another inverted plate or cardboard circle over the pudding. Again, invert the whole thing.

Remove both the top plate and the piece of wax paper, and the pudding will be right side up. The pudding will be very soft, with some syrupy liquid collecting on the plate. Allow the pudding to cool about 10 to 15 minutes, then cut into wedges and serve with a dollop of pear brandy hard sauce (recipe follows) on top of each wedge. The hard sauce should start to melt a little as you serve the warm pudding.

PEAR BRANDY HARD SAUCE

MAKES ABOUT 1 CUP

1½ sticks (¾ cup) unsalted butter, softened

1½ cups confectioners' sugar

3 tablespoons Clear Creek Pear Brandy (or other good-quality brandy)

A STEP AHEAD:

For the HARD SAUCE, in the bowl of an electric mixer using the paddle, or in a bowl with an electric hand mixer, cream the butter. Gradually beat in the confectioners' sugar. Add the brandy and beat until fluffy. Serve at room temperature. Hard sauce keeps for several days covered in the refrigerator. Bring it to room temperature before serving.

If you'd like to make the pudding up to one day ahead of time, unmold it onto something that can go into the oven, such as a cardboard circle or the bottom of a springform pan. Allow the pudding to cool completely, then wrap in plastic wrap and leave at room temperature. Before serving, unwrap the cake and transfer it to a baking sheet. Loosely cover the pudding with foil and reheat in a 350 degree oven until warm, about 15 to 20 minutes.

HOSHIGAKI

The traditional Japanese method of drying Hachiya persimmons, known as hoshigaki, came to the United States with Japanese American farmers, but the technique disappeared from commercial production for decades. Hoshigaki produces a succulent smooth texture with an outstanding persimmon–gingerbread taste that is not overly sweet despite the light frost of natural sugar on the surface.

To dry persimmons successfully in this way, you need cold, dry winter weather, a place with dry active air circulation, and a lot of patience. Peel the firm Hachiya persimmon and cut off the calyx except for a small circle around the stem. Hang the persimmon by its stem for three to seven days. When a skin forms on the persimmon, it is time to massage the persimmon. Yep, massage the persimmon. It needs to be gently but firmly rolled and massaged to break up the hard inner pulp. Continue massaging every three to five days for three to five weeks. When the pulp sets and you can no longer roll it, the persimmon is finally dried and rubbed to perfection and the natural sugars have come to the outside of the fruit, leaving the surface with a sweet, even dusting of fine powdery white sugar.

10

Stone Fruits:

Apricot *(Prunus armeniaca)*
Peach *(Prunus persica)*
and Nectarine *(Prunus persica nectarina)*

If only! It would be a dream come true if apricots, peaches, and nectarines could be reliably grown in all of the Pacific maritime climates. These fruits tend to need more summer heat, and a more predictable spring demarcation, than most of our regions can provide. Moreover, the experts say that wherever these trees are grown, they are the weaklings of the fruit world and need more fussy care than some other fruit trees.

People are usually willing to put a lot of effort into what they love, and if you love these stone fruits, it will all be worthwhile to get a tree-ripened apricot, peach, or nectarine from your very own tree.

Apricot

Beyond the fruit the beauty of the apricot tree with its graceful canopy and its delicate green leaves lined with enunciated red veins is reason enough to plant it.

Most of the apricot varieties we plant today are offspring of those planted in the 1800s by the Spanish missionaries. Apricots are rich in beta carotene, and a dried apricot has a whopping 40 percent sugar content. What you may have heard about apricot kernels is true—each one contains a very tiny amount of cyanide, so savor the fruit and toss the pit.

Apricots can grow to be large sturdy trees, and they bloom and set fruit enthusiastically when all goes well—here we are mostly talking about the weather. Apricots have low chilling requirements, which means that they are all too ready to pop out blossoms during a warm spell in late winter, not realizing that the vagaries of our weather up and down the coast could include a cold spell following springlike days and might even include frost. The blossoms that explode on warm days have their promise crushed if it turns cold again, so choosing a variety that has been developed to bloom later in the spring is most important if you want fruit production in the more northern zones. If you are lucky enough to have a sheltered warm spot, few trees will give you as much pleasure as an apricot.

If you are far enough inland to get reliable summer heat, apricots will thrive, but they need more heat than many coastal gardens can provide. If you see or hear of one growing and producing well in your area, it would be worth your time to see if you can pay a visit to ask questions of the caretaker and closely observe the conditions that make the tree happy. With those tips in hand, you can try to offer your apricot a similar environment.

Apricots like regular water to develop good size and taste. You can test by digging down about six inches to see if your soil is slightly moist. If dryness meets your spade at inch six, it is time to water. Using drip emitters in the perimeter of the canopy is an excellent way to water a larger tree, but for a small tree you can build up a six-inch-high berm around the drip line of the tree, fill the basin with water, and let it soak in. Mulch will help to slow moisture loss.

Some gardeners insist you should hand-thin your baby apricots if there are too many of them, and others say that the way to limit overproduction is through pruning. If, even with your efforts at pruning, your tree still has produced too much fruit, help it out in midspring by taking off enough fruits to leave two to four inches between each one. Apricots bear on short spurs on the previous year's growth—also known as second-year wood. The spurs produce for about four years. When pruning, preserve enough of these that you will get a crop the next year and at the same time create new growth. Prune back most of the leaders of last year's growth and cut the current season's leaders back by half. Apricots are best maintained in an open vase shapes with no central trunk. Take out any branches that are crossing, or growing vertically, and thin out branches to make sure sunlight can reach the middle of the tree. Summer pruning is best done on dry days after harvest.

Let your fruit ripen on the tree. An apricot picked before it is ripe will soften while sitting on your counter, but it won't develop any more sweetness. Your apricot is ready to pick when the color is golden with a rose blush, has a rich apricot fragrance, and yields to gentle pressure. Apricots can be kept in the refrigerator for a few days but, to bring out the best taste, let each fruit come back to room temperature before eating. Waiting till apricots are tree ripened may mean doing battle with the critters who want your harvest, but it will be worth it when you take that first sun-warmed bite.

Best Bets for Apricots

The following lists tell which apricots are suited to their respective zones. There might be more that would grow well in each zone; however, these varieties are the ones that experts most highly recommend.

BEST BETS FOR ZONE 8B

No apricot variety is a sure thing in this coastal zone but if you have a warm microclimate in your yard, and a taste for great apricots, try one of these:

HARGLOW. This was developed in Ontario, Canada, and the secret for its success in the Pacific coastal zone is that it is a late-blooming variety that, hopefully, blooms after the spring cold weather is really over. The sweet, firm, flavorful fruit is a medium-sized bright-orange, sometimes blushed red. It is productive and disease resistant. Self-fertile.

PUGET GOLD. This is the most productive and disease-resistant variety for this region. It was developed in Western Washington at Washington State University and will bloom and set fruit even in frosty spring weather. Beautiful blossoms in March lead to large and flavorful ripe fruit in August. Less than twelve to fifteen feet tall when fully grown, it likes well-drained soil in a sunny place. Self-fertile.

BEST BET FOR ZONE 8A

PUGET GOLD. Developed in Western Washington at Washington State University, this apricot will bloom and set fruit even in frosty spring weather. Beautiful blossoms in March lead to large and flavorful ripe fruit in August. Less than twelve to fifteen feet tall when fully grown, it likes well-drained soil in a sunny place. Self-fertile.

BEST BETS FOR ZONE 9B

BLENHEIM (OR ROYAL BLENHEIM). This one has a classically delicious apricot flavor in an aromatic medium-sized fruit. It blooms early and is ready to harvest in early to mid-summer. Self-fertile.

TILTON. A little later ripening version of the Blenheim, it is a heavy producer of medium-sized richly flavored fruits that are the best apricots for canning and excellent fresh or dried too. Self-fertile.

PUGET GOLD. This disease-resistant variety will bloom and set fruit even in frosty spring weather. Beautiful blossoms in March lead to large and flavorful ripe fruit in August. Less than twelve to fifteen feet tall when fully grown, it likes well-drained soil in a sunny place. Self-fertile.

BEST BETS FOR ZONE 9A

BLENHEIM (OR ROYAL BLENHEIM). This one has a classically delicious apricot flavor in an aromatic medium-sized fruit. It blooms early and is ready to harvest in early to mid-summer. Self-fertile.

TILTON. A little later ripening version of the Blenheim, it is a heavy producer of medium-sized richly flavored fruits that are the best apricots for canning and excellent fresh or dried too. Self-fertile.

CANADIAN WHITE BLENHEIM. This new variety has extremely sweet white, firm textured flesh. Tops in taste tests, but it takes a few years to start bearing well. Needs a late-flowering variety such as Wenatchee Moorepark to pollenize it.

WENATCHEE MOOREPARK. A good apricot to grow where spring rains and late frosts limit most apricots, this flavorful, large, oval fruit is good out of hand as well as for drying and canning. Ripens July through August. Self-fertile.

BEST BETS FOR ZONE 10

BLENHEIM (OR ROYAL BLENHEIM). This one has a classically delicious apricot flavor in an aromatic medium-sized fruit. It blooms early and is ready to harvest in early to mid-summer. Self-fertile.

ROYAL ROSA. A sweet, low-acid fruit with good flavor, this extremely vigorous tree starts bearing young and is more disease resistant than many other apricot varieties. Harvest begins in early to mid-May! Self-fertile.

GOLD KIST. The rich flavor of this fruit makes it ideal for cooking, drying, and canning. This is an excellent choice for warm winter areas. It produces fragrant blossoms in the spring and is ready to harvest in late May. Don't forget to thin the fruit for maximum size and fruit quality. Self-fertile.

THE TRICK TO DRYING APRICOTS

In a banner year, drying apricots is not complicated. To start the drying process, wash the fruit, cut in two, and remove the pit. Then, and this is important, press the skin side of the apricot in, so that the flesh side is pushed out. This will help in the drying process. Soak the apricot halves in a mixture of ¼ cup lemon or lime juice to 1 cup water for 5 minutes to keep the apricots from turning brown as they dry. If you are not using a dehydrator, spread the fruit on a baking sheet so that pieces are not touching. Put it in an oven set to 135 degrees Fahrenheit till they dry but are still pliable. Check them often to determine the degree of dryness.

Peach and Nectarine

It's easy to see why calling someone a peach is a compliment. Peaches bring us the true essence of summer in a soft-skinned package.

Peach varieties are either cling or freestone, depending on whether the flesh clings to the seed or the seed comes free easily. Peaches can be yellow or white inside, although both colors usually have some red on their skin. Peaches with white flesh are very sweet and low acid, while the yellow ones give some tang along with the sweet. A nectarine is really just a slightly tangier, smooth-skinned variety of a peach. It has a recessive gene that gives it the smooth nectarine skin instead of fuzzier peach skin. Peaches and nectarines are genetically so similar that growing a nectarine tree is essentially the same as growing a peach.

The key for any hope of success with peaches and nectarines in the maritime climate lies with your choice of variety. They are happiest with hot weather and clear skies while they grow, and this makes them very iffy for gardeners whose summer skies are often lined with clouds or fog and much more reliable for gardeners farther inland. On the other side of the seasonal chart, most peaches and nectarines need some serious cold to send out leaves at the right time in the spring. Low-chill varieties will be your allies here.

After you have chosen the correct variety for your climate and found the perfect sunny nook to plant it in, pay attention to your dirt. Peaches and nectarines like good drainage and loose, loamy soil so much that they won't even grow in heavy clay soil that doesn't drain well. Plant on a slope if your soil tends to be on the clay side, or build up a small hill of good soil to plant your tree on.

Because peaches and nectarines are self-fertile, you only need one peach or one nectarine tree in your yard. They grow so vigorously that they can need some additional nitrogen. Dig some fish emulsion or compost into the soil under the drip line once in the early spring and again in early summer.

Peaches and nectarines often set way too much fruit for each one to be able to grow to its intended size. Even if the idea of lots and lots of small peaches or nectarines appeals to you, the tree limbs will groan and could break with the weight of all the developing fruit. When the fruitlets are slightly larger than a quarter, hand-thin some of them until they are six to ten inches apart. As for apricots, it's not good to just sit back and watch your tree grow; it needs careful pruning. Prune your peach or nectarine tree to an open vase shape, with three to five branches coming out of a main trunk two to three feet above the ground, or train it as a fruit "bush."

Prune lightly in the winter each year to take out branches that grow downward, across, or straight up. When the tree is about the size you want it, but no more than twelve feet tall, you can start pruning more heavily, taking off a third of the old bearing branches each year because the new growth will give you the most peaches. An established tree will send out up to thirty inches of new growth in one season. If you are fertilizing regularly and your tree isn't giving you a good crop, it may be a sign that you are not pruning off enough. Genetic dwarf trees, though, do not need this kind of pruning. They can be espaliered and will also do well grown in containers.

The time to pick your peach or nectarine is when it is firm-ripe but not yet soft-ripe. You may have to do a little experimenting by tasting fruit at different stages so you can discover the best picking time for your tree. Some late-maturing varieties are better when they are harvested a little on the firmer side and set out to ripen on the counter. When picking, pull gently but firmly straight down from the branch with the sides of your fingers. Really, even pulling with the fingertips could put small bruises in the flesh. Some people say peaches will ripen and get sweeter if stored in a paper bag for a day or two, while others say they will get softer but not sweeter. With your own peach tree, you can do some experimentation and become the expert on this question. Peaches and nectarines do not store well. Keep them at room temperature, separated slightly from each other for air circulation, for three or four days and in the refrigerator in a plastic bag for a day or two more. After that, it's either eat or preserve.

Best Bets for Peaches

The following lists tell which peaches and nectarines are suited to their respective zones. There may be more that would grow well in each zone; however, these varieties are the ones that experts most highly recommend.

BEST BET FOR ZONE 8B

Named for horticulturalist Herb Frost, this variety has nothing to do with frosty weather.

FROST. It is a flavorful, yellow-fleshed peach with greenish-yellow tangy fruit that can be good for fresh eating but best for canning. They may never match the quality of peaches grown in a more favorable climate, but you can get a fresh peach experience. Self-fertile and good leaf curl–resistant choice.

BEST BETS FOR ZONE 8A

OREGON CURL FREE. "Curl free" is what it is all about in this climate. When established, this variety produces good crops of large, tasty, sweet, and juicy orange-yellow fruit that ripen in mid-August and are great for eating out of hand, baking, and preserving. Self-fertile.

CHARLOTTE. This variety has good disease resistance and bears good crops of delicious orange-red semi-freestone sweet fruit. Self-fertile.

Q1-8. An early-ripening white-flesh variety, this peach was discovered in the state of Washington. It has showy pink blossoms in the spring, followed by juicy, sweetly flavored, semi-freestone fruit. It has been compared to the taste of a Babcock. Great for fresh eating. Self-fertile and very resistant to peach leaf curl.

BEST BET FOR ZONE 9B

FROST. This peach is named for horticulturalist Herb Frost. It is a flavorful, yellow-fleshed, midseason peach with greenish-yellow tangy fruit that can be good for fresh eating but best for canning. It is a reliably heavy producer. Self-fertile and very resistant to peach leaf curl.

BEST BETS FOR ZONE 9A

ELBERTAS (FAY, KIM, GLEASON). Any of the freestone Elbertas are good choices, with the Fay Elberta being the best for flavor and texture. All are great for fresh eating, cooking, and canning. Self-fertile.

RED HAVEN. The skin is a brilliant red over yellow, and the flesh is yellow with a bit of red near the pit. This very tasty semi-freestone is juicy and sweet with a smooth texture. The vigorous tree will produce an early to midseason harvest that is great for fresh eating as well as desserts. Self-fertile.

FAIRTIME. This variety produces abundant crops of red fruit with yellow, good-flavored flesh and a smooth melting texture that is best for fresh eating. This late-season freestone variety needs heavy pruning. The flowers are large and showy. Self-fertile.

BEST BETS FOR ZONE 10

KIM ELBERTA. A yellow freestone with red streaks over greenish-yellow fuzzy skin with yellow flesh and firm, fine texture. Also known as July Elberta, this tree bears prolifically, and you may need to do a little extra thinning. Self-fertile.

BABCOCK. The white flesh is tender, juicy, and sweet, with a bit of tang, and the skin has little fuzz. Thinning the fruit is essential to get the size and quality you want from this early-season variety. The spreading, vigorous tree is self-fertile.

HONEY BABE. You'll get an early harvest of large fruit with deep red-over-yellow skin and orange flesh dusted with red. The flavor is excellent, and the tree is an attractive genetic dwarf that blooms beautifully in spring. Self-fertile.

VETERAN. Good for the coast because it sets fruit in less-than-ideal conditions, this medium-sized fruit is yellow with a slight red blush with firm, juicy, yellow flesh. This freestone variety is low acid and easy to peel. Self-fertile.

Best Bets for Nectarines

BEST BET FOR ZONE 8B

There are really no nectarines that thrive in this coastal zone. The Hardired is the best bet, but it is susceptible to peach leaf curl.

HARDIRED. It can bear large quantities of sweet, tasty, yellow-fleshed nectarines in early August, with showy pink flowers in the spring. Self-fertile.

BEST BET FOR ZONE 8A

KREIBICH. A sweet and delicious white-fleshed nectarine of medium size discovered in Western Washington by Roland Kreibich, it reliably produces bright-red, sweet, smooth-skinned fruit. Has some resistance to peach leaf curl. Self-fertile.

BEST BETS FOR ZONE 9B

HARKO. The best nectarine variety for the coastal areas in this zone. It bears large quantities of red-skinned tasty fruit with yellow flesh in early August. The beautiful spreading tree has showy pink flowers in the spring and has some disease resistance. This freestone variety is self-fertile.

SNOW QUEEN. A very early-season, sweet, and juicy nectarine, great for mild winter regions, the Snow Queen produces an abundant harvest of red-skinned and white-fleshed fruits in late June. Self-fertile.

BEST BETS FOR ZONE 9A

FANTASIA. This variety will give you large, oval fruit with a sweet and tangy flavor while firm-ripe in midseason; later harvests will give you sweetness with rich flavor. The skin is mostly bright-red over yellow, and the freestone flesh is firm and smooth. The vigorous trees have showy flowers. Self-fertile.

FLAVORTOP. This freestone variety has red skin dusted with yellow, and the firm, juicy flesh is golden-yellow with red. The flavor is excellent, and the tree is vigorous with showy flowers and abundant crops in midseason. Self-fertile.

ARCTIC BLAZE. This very tasty, low-acid, large white fruit has rich flavor and firm texture. It has red- and cream-colored skin and is very sweet and soft when ripe. Self-fertile.

BEST BETS FOR ZONE 10

ARCTIC STAR. This early-season, really sweet and super-tasty, low-acid, semi-freestone has dark-red skin and snow-white flesh. Self-fertile.

HEAVENLY WHITE. This variety gives you a rich, complex, aromatic flavor with great acid–sugar balance in a large, firm, but juicy freestone fruit. The flesh is white, and the skin is red and cream. Harvest in midseason. Self-fertile.

THE GLORIOUS APRICOT HARVEST

Most gardeners who grow apricot trees are hard pressed to do anything with the harvest other than to eat every single one straight off the branches, but preserves, cobblers, tarts, and all manner of desserts can be made with apricots. Apricots go well with chicken and pork, and nonfat cream cheese–stuffed apricot halves with a sprinkle of pistachios are good as an appetizer or light dessert. Add apricots, wine, sugar, and a little vanilla extract to lend great flavor to brandy or vodka.

AGED PECORINO WITH WATERCRESS AND ROASTED APRICOT–MARCONA ALMOND PURÉE

Adapted from a recipe featured in Ethan Stowell's New Italian Kitchen, *this dish makes a fabulous first course. Alternatively, you can shake it up and serve it after dinner as both salad and cheese course in place of dessert, the way Chef Stowell prefers. The earthiness of the apricots is a perfect match for salty, aged pecorino. Peruse your local cheese shop or importer for your favorite variety, or try a local cheesemaker's version. Pecorino hails from Tuscany, and Chef Stowell recommends drinking a Tuscan white with this dish. If serving as a first course, grilled bread makes a nice accompaniment.*

MAKES 4 SERVINGS

½ cup Marcona almonds

3 tablespoons plus 2 teaspoons extra-virgin olive oil (for drizzling)

4 ripe apricots, halved and pitted

1 teaspoon sugar

2 bunches watercress, washed and patted dry

1 tablespoon Chianti vinegar

Salt and cracked pepper

8 ounces aged sheep's milk pecorino (about 2 ounces per person)

Preheat the oven to 350 degrees F. Spread the Marcona almonds on a baking sheet and toast lightly in the oven until fragrant, watching them carefully to ensure they don't burn. Remove to a plate to cool. Increase the oven temperature to 400 degrees F.

Line a baking sheet with a silicone liner or parchment paper and drizzle with about 2 teaspoons olive oil. Roll the apricot halves in the olive oil on the baking sheet. Place them cut sides down and sprinkle with the sugar. Bake for 15 minutes, or until they have caramelized and collapsed. Remove and cool to room temperature.

Combine the roasted apricots and almonds in a food processor and process until the texture is silky smooth. To ensure the apricot-almond purée is free of any chunks, pass it through a tamis or fine-mesh sieve, discarding any solids.

Pick off the most perfect watercress leaves, discarding any older tougher leaves and stems. In a large bowl, toss the watercress first with 3 tablespoons olive oil, then the Chianti vinegar. Season with salt and cracked pepper to taste.

Using a spoon, spread out roughly 2 tablespoons of the apricot-almond purée alongside the watercress salad and nestle individual portions of the pecorino on each of four plates. Drizzle with a bit of extra-virgin olive oil.

DEHYDRATE FRUIT IN YOUR CAR!

Fruit drying can be done without electricity by placing a tray of fruit in your car on a hot day. You will get preserved fruit and for a bonus—a great smelling car! A thermometer and occasional monitoring will let you know if the fruit is getting hot enough or too hot. You want enough heat so that the fruit will dry within thirty-six hours to prevent molding, but not so much heat that the fruit gets cooked. An air temperature right around 135 degrees Fahrenheit is best. Too much heat can easily be moderated by opening the window as much as necessary to get the correct temperature. Even if they are sliced, some thicker fruits, like figs, may need more than one day in a sunny vehicle.

Here's how it works: Spread the sliced or quartered fruit on parchment paper on a baking sheet. Make sure the pieces aren't touching each other, and put the baking sheet in the back window or dashboard of your car parked where it will get sun all day. Store the dried fruit in a tightly closed jar kept in a cool dry place for up to two years.

POACHED APRICOTS WITH HAZELNUT FINANCIERS

Luxurious poached apricots spiced with vanilla and orange pair perfectly with nutty hazelnut financiers, addictive individual cakes rich with browned butter. Pastry Chef Aaron Heath of Araxi in Whistler, B.C., plates the apricots and cakes on apricot coulis (or purée). Rest assured, they are equally delicious if presented more casually. The poached apricots are also fabulous on their own, perhaps topped with a scoop of ice cream. MAKES 6 SERVINGS

Recipe Note: These cakes require two pieces of special equipment, though they are straightforward to prepare. You will need a scale to weigh the ingredients and also small molds to bake the cakes. Chef Heath uses a mini-savarin mold, which produces cakes that look a bit like doughnuts. There are also silicone molds in a variety of shapes designed just for financiers, though a mini muffin tin will also work. Just adjust the baking time accordingly and test for doneness as instructed. To make simple syrup, combine 1 cup water and 1 cup sugar in a small saucepan. Bring to a boil to dissolve the sugar and let cool.

POACHED APRICOTS

⅞ cup brandy

1 cup simple syrup (see recipe note)

⅔ cup white wine

1 vanilla bean, pod split and seeds scraped

Two 2-inch pieces orange zest

12 whole ripe apricots, skin on

HAZELNUT FINANCIERS

2 tablespoons granulated sugar

2 sticks (1 cup) unsalted butter, cut into 1-inch cubes

3 ounces ground hazelnuts plus 1 tablespoon (for garnish)

10 ounces confectioners' sugar, sifted

3 ounces all-purpose flour, sifted

To make the poaching liquid, combine the brandy, simple syrup, white wine, vanilla, and orange zest in a medium saucepan and bring to a boil on high heat. Remove from heat and keep warm.

Fill a large bowl with ice water. Set a medium-sized pot to boil. Using a sharp knife, score the bottom of each apricot with a small X. Immerse the apricots in the boiling water for 15 seconds, or until the skin starts to loosen. Using a slotted spoon, plunge the apricots into the ice water to stop the cooking and allow them to cool. Remove the apricots from the ice water, pat them dry, and discard the skins.

Cut the apricots in half, discard the pits, and add the fruit to the reserved brandied poaching liquid. Return this mixture to low heat and simmer gently for 5 to 8 minutes, or until the apricots are soft. Remove from the heat. Using a slotted spoon, transfer the apricots to a clean bowl and refrigerate for 30 minutes until chilled. Strain the poaching liquid through a fine-mesh sieve and reserve it for the hazelnut financiers.

To make the FINANCIERS, lightly grease six 2-ounce savarin molds and sprinkle with the granulated sugar. Arrange the molds on a baking sheet.

Place a small stainless-steel bowl in the freezer. Melt the butter in a medium-sized saucepan on high heat, whisking constantly. The

1 vanilla bean, seeds scraped
  and pod discarded
8 ounces egg whites (from
  7 to 8 eggs), room
  temperature
Reserved apricot poaching
  liquid
1 cup apricot coulis (optional,
  for garnish)
6 sprigs fresh mint, for
  garnish

butter will foam and then subside. Continue cooking the butter on high until it becomes golden brown and gives off a nutty aroma. (This is a brown butter, or *beurre noisette*.) Remove the brown butter from the heat and transfer it to the chilled bowl to stop the cooking. Allow the butter to cool to room temperature, stirring frequently so it remains smooth.

In a large bowl, combine the hazelnuts with the confectioners' sugar, flour, and vanilla. Using a rubber spatula, gradually stir in the egg whites until they are fully combined. Fold in the reserved brown butter and mix well. Refrigerate the batter for 1 hour, until it is chilled.

Preheat the oven to 350 degrees F. Transfer the batter to a piping bag fitted with a wide nozzle or a resealable plastic bag with the corner cut off. Fill the savarin molds two-thirds full (or just spoon the batter into the individual molds). Bake for 6 minutes, then turn the molds around to ensure even cooking and bake for 3 to 5 minutes more, or until the cakes are golden brown. The cakes are cooked when a skewer or toothpick inserted into the thickest part comes out clean. Remove the financiers from the oven.

Line a baking sheet with parchment paper. Invert the cakes onto the baking sheet. While they are still warm, briefly dip each financier into the reserved apricot poaching liquid.

Spoon a sixth of the apricot coulis into the center of each plate. Top with a financier, then arrange two poached apricot halves on each cake. Sprinkle each serving with ground hazelnuts and garnish with a sprig of mint.

THE GLORIOUS PEACH AND NECTARINE HARVEST

Peach or nectarine cobblers, ice cream, crisp, grilled peaches with or without balsamic vinegar, broiled peaches, baked peaches stuffed with custard or cookies or graham crackers, peach and pineapple juice, peach or nectarine daiquiris, jams, pies, sliced over cereal. . . . The list of culinary treats for the versatile peach and nectarine is maybe not endless but definitely long.

GRILLED PROSCIUTTO-WRAPPED PEACH SALAD

Chef Lizzie Binder of San Francisco's Bar Bambino, an Italian eatery in the Mission district, is a happy and prolific backyard orchardist at her own home in Napa. The "mini orchard" of pomegranate, nectarine, Meyer lemon, orange, grapefruit, lime, pear, apple, Damson plum, fig, and avocado trees are a constant inspiration, as is one peach tree, which Chef Binder reports as producing the best peaches she has ever eaten. This exquisite summer dish makes the most of perfect peaches. Chef Binder uses La Quercia Rossa, a domestically produced heirloom-breed prosciutto, to wrap the peaches. As with all recipes with precious few ingredients, make sure you use the best you can afford. MAKES 4 SERVINGS

2 firm, ripe freestone peaches
12 thin slices of prosciutto
4 handfuls of dandelion
  greens, washed and picked
Good extra-virgin olive oil
Aged balsamic vinegar
Salt and freshly ground
  black pepper
Parmigiano-Reggiano

Heat a gas or charcoal grill to medium-high heat. Peel and halve each peach, then cut each half into three wedges. Wrap each peach wedge with thinly sliced prosciutto.

If the dandelion greens are small and tender just wash and pat dry. If they are larger and more unruly, soak in cold water for a half hour to remove some of the bitterness. Spin them or lay them on kitchen towels to dry, then chop into smaller more manageable pieces.

Grill the wrapped peaches on a clean grill, until crispy and marked to a light golden brown. While the peaches are grilling, toss the dandelion greens with a drizzle of extra-virgin olive oil and aged balsamic vinegar. Season to taste with salt and ground black pepper. Serve the salad with the crispy warm peach wedges. Shave Parmigiano-Reggiano over the top.

NECTARINE, BOYSENBERRY, AND ALMOND CRISP

Fresh from Portland's Cory Schreiber and Julie Richardson comes this celebration of the nectarine, so often overlooked for that flashy peach. The recipe comes from their cookbook, Rustic Fruit Desserts, *chock full of brilliant ideas for using your backyard bounty. Because nectarines and boysenberries both have a high water content and release moisture as they bake, cornstarch is added to the filling and baking in a wide dish encourages evaporation. While almond is their first choice to complement the fruits' commingled flavors, you could use walnuts or hazelnuts as well. Top with homemade vanilla ice cream or lightly sweetened whipped cream.* **MAKES 8 TO 10 SERVINGS**

CRISP TOPPING
1¼ cups all-purpose flour
¾ cup granulated sugar
1 teaspoon fine sea salt
1 stick (½ cup) cold unsalted
    butter, cut into 6 cubes
¾ cup sliced almonds, toasted

FRUIT FILLING
½ cup granulated sugar
2 tablespoons cornstarch
½ teaspoon fine sea salt
6 nectarines, each cut into
    10 to 12 slices
1 dry pint (2 cups)
    fresh boysenberries
1 tablespoon vanilla extract

Preheat the oven to 400 degrees F. Grease a 3-quart baking dish.

To make the CRISP TOPPING, stir together the flour, sugar, and sea salt in a bowl. Add the butter and toss until evenly coated. Using your fingertips or a pastry blender, cut in the butter until the mixture resembles crumbs. Pour in the almonds and mix gently; try not to break the almond slices. Put the topping in the freezer while you prepare the fruit filling.

To make the FRUIT FILLING, rub the sugar, cornstarch, and sea salt together in a large bowl. Add the nectarines and boysenberries, toss until evenly coated, then gently stir in the vanilla extract.

Pour the filling into the prepared baking dish and scatter the topping over the fruit. Bake for 45 to 55 minutes, or until the topping is golden and the fruit is bubbling. Cool for 30 minutes before serving.

The crisp will keep on the counter, wrapped in plastic wrap, for up to three days. Reheat in a 325 degree oven for 10 minutes before serving.

PEACH AND BRANDY SOUP
WITH SOUR CREAM ICE CREAM

Cold soups are an exquisite way to capture the essence of your backyard fruit and make for a refreshing first course or dessert in the heat of summer. Here Aaron Heath of Araxi in Whistler, B.C., accents the ripest peaches with a touch of brandy. The sour cream ice cream is worth a try on its own and could turn a simple bowl of cut fruit into an event, but why not pull out all the stops and prepare the dish as Chef Heath intended? The peach purée may be made up to three days ahead; store in an airtight container in the refrigerator. MAKES 8 SERVINGS

PEACH PURÉE
5 pounds whole ripe peaches
2 vanilla beans, pods split and
seeds scraped
Juice of 1 lemon

PEACH AND BRANDY SOUP
½ cup brandy
1 vanilla bean, pod split and
seeds scraped
¼ cup superfine (caster) sugar
6 black peppercorns, crushed
2 cups chilled peach purée
(recipe above)
½ cup Champagne or sweet
sparkling wine
Juice of 1½ lemons
2 ripe peaches, blanched and
peeled, for garnish
8 sprigs fresh mint or anise
hyssop, for garnish

SOUR CREAM ICE CREAM
4 cups sour cream (do not use
low-fat or no-fat varieties)
1¼ cups granulated sugar
Juice of 2 lemons
⅓ cup heavy cream

Using a clean, dry towel, rub the fuzz off the peaches but leave the skins on. Cut in half and discard the pits. Place the fruit and the vanilla in a large saucepan and cook on medium-low heat, stirring frequently, until the peaches are just soft, about 10 minutes. Stir in the lemon juice. Discard the vanilla pods.

Transfer the mixture to a food processor and purée until smooth, or blend with a hand-held blender. Pass the peach purée through a fine-mesh sieve into a clean bowl and refrigerate until chilled, about 1 hour.

For the SOUP, combine the brandy, vanilla, sugar, and black peppercorns in a small saucepan on low heat. Bring to a boil and simmer gently for 2 to 3 minutes, then remove from the heat and allow to cool. Strain into a clean bowl and discard the solids.

Pour the peach purée into a bowl. Stir in the brandy mixture, Champagne, and two-thirds of the lemon juice until well mixed. Refrigerate for 1 hour.

To make the ICE CREAM, combine the sour cream, sugar, lemon juice, and heavy cream in a large bowl and whisk until smooth. Allow the mixture to stand for 30 minutes to dissolve the sugar. Transfer the mixture to an ice cream maker and process.

Before serving, place eight small bowls in the freezer. Halve the blanched peaches and discard the pits. Cut the peaches into 1-inch pieces. In a small bowl, toss the peach cubes with the remaining lemon juice to prevent oxidization.

Divide the peaches among the chilled bowls. Ladle the soup on top and garnish with a scoop of sour cream ice cream and a sprig of mint. Serve immediately.

Cherry

Sweet Cherry (*Prunus avium*)
and Sour Cherry (*Prunus cerasus*)

Cherry trees in bloom have ignited creativity in humans for thousands of years in paintings, poems, songs, and celebrations and with plenty of good reason. The clouds of delicate blossoms, though ephemeral, are lovely. Most of the varieties that bloom so profusely, though, are not grown for their fruit production. In fact, many are completely fruitless. The varieties we grow for their fruit crops flower beautifully too, just not as heavily as the ornamentals.

There are two main types of eating cherries—the sweet and the sour (tart). The sweet ones are usually found in the produce section of the grocery store, and the sours are often preserved in jars or cans ready for pie and dessert making. For both types the fruit usually appears about two months after bloom, and all cherry trees can take as little as three or as much as six years to start to bear fruit. Maritime cherries are happiest with an application of spring compost and mulch.

Sweet varieties, although they can deliver heaven in small packages, have more delicate constitutions than the sour (tart) varieties. The sweets need light-to-medium, deep, loamy soil and prefer lots of chilling hours. They are attractive to insects and fungi, especially in foggy coastal areas. Rain at harvest time can cause cracking, too much summer heat will reduce the fruit quality, and hot summers can produce "double" or spurred fruit in the next year (although that particular problem will not seem like a big deal to most backyard fruit growers). Regular deep watering is necessary as cherry trees are sensitive to drought, but the soil has to drain well so roots aren't standing in water and inviting root rot. On the other hand, the sweet cherry's late-blooming flowers are not so susceptible to being killed by spring frosts as the sour (tart) varieties.

Sweet cherries grow on upright trees without many side branches when they are young. Cut back at the outward-growing buds to force branches to head in the direction you want them to go. Cherries produce fruit on long-lived, short spurs right off the older main branches, so they need less pruning than other fruit trees. In fact, cherry trees dislike hard pruning, so don't take off too much. When the trees are established, just prune to cut out any weak or crossing branches and, to keep them from getting too tall, cut back to strong lateral (side) branches.

There are sweet cherries that are self-fertile, but many sweet varieties need a pollenizing tree nearby and are very choosy about which other variety they will match up with for pollination. Check carefully before you buy your trees to make sure they are either self-fertile varieties or that you are buying two compatible pollenizers. Sometimes you can find or order a tree that has a pollenizing variety grafted onto it—the best idea ever. If you get two trees, it is essential that the two have overlapping blooming times.

The sour varieties, which are sometimes called "the wilder cousins," are usually grown for dessert making and for canning. There are two types of sour cherries—the most common has translucent yellow flesh and clear juice, and the other has bright-red flesh and dark-red juice. The second is the one we usually think of as a pie cherry. The sour cherry is much more forgiving than the sweet on many counts. It can thrive in poor soil and withstand heat, cold, and drought better than many other fruit trees and has having fewer insect and fungal problems. However, even the iron-tough sour cherry will not tolerate waterlogged soil, and because it blooms early in the spring, it is easily damaged by spring frosts. Sour cherries will pollenize sweet cherries, but having a spring when both types blossom at the same time is not to be depended upon.

The sour cherry is best trained to a vase shape or a fruit "bush." It spreads more than a sweet cherry and creates good distance between its main branches without much help from you. All you really need to do with an established sour cherry is to thin the excess new interior shoots. It bears on fruiting spurs and also on one-year-old side branches. The trees do tend to sucker, so be sure to cut these off from the base of the tree.

Because all cherries need significant cold time, after a mild winter your tree might produce some fruit but rarely basketful. If it happens to rain as the cherry gets close to harvest time, many varieties will split since most of a juicy cherry's flesh is made up of water surrounded by a tight skin. Your best and maybe only recourse if this happens is to harvest all the fruit quickly after the rain and refrigerate all of it. Cherries keep about a week in the refrigerator. If you have a large harvest, plan on celebrating exuberantly with friends or preserving what you can't eat in seven or eight days.

How birds love cherries—sweet or sour—and will compete mightily to score your crop! If you keep your tree small, netting the whole thing is the best answer to winning the bird battle, but if you have let your tree grow to its full glory, you will need to resort to some scare tactics. Tie Mylar strips or aluminum pie pans on the outer branches. Blow-up snakes or big eyeball balloons or fake owls can be effective deterrents if you change their placement often. Some gardeners suggest planting a mulberry tree along with a cherry as a sacrifice crop to the birds, as the mulberry fruits about the same time as the cherry and birds seem to prefer the smaller mulberries. But if you also love mulberries, this would be a difficult choice.

The litany of cautions for producing your own cherries may seem daunting, but those who get any kind of harvest from their cherry tree, even if some years are not as good as others, say it is worth every bit of effort.

Best Bets for Cherries

The following lists tell which cherries are suited to their respective zones. There may be more that would grow well in each zone; however, these cherry varieties are the ones that experts most highly recommend.

BEST BETS FOR ZONE 8B

LAPINS. This sweet purplish-black cherry is a favorite of the commercial growers. A productive and easy-to-grow variety from Canada that is crack resistant and flavorful. It will ripen late season in this zone. Self-fertile.

TEHRANIVEE. This sweet cross of Van and Stella cherries was developed by and named for Gus Tehrani of Ontario. This large, firm cherry with excellent flavor has an unusual mahogany-color skin with black-red juice. Self-fertile.

BEST BETS FOR ZONE 8A

GOLD. This sweet and flavorful, bright-yellow cherry is a good pollenizer for other cherries. Reliable and productive, it is easy to grow in this zone, as it is disease resistant and resists cracking if it rains. Needs another cherry for pollination.

COMPACT STELLA. This sweet cherry tree can easily be maintained at six to ten feet in height, and it is an ideal choice for the small backyard. It bears large, juicy, almost black fruit of excellent quality. It starts bearing at a younger age than most cherry varieties. Self-fertile.

LAPINS. This sweet purplish-black cherry is a favorite of the commercial growers. It is a productive and easy-to-grow variety from Canada that is crack resistant and flavorful. It will ripen late season in this zone. Self-fertile.

BEST BETS FOR ZONE 9B

STELLA. Bearing sweet, tasty, juicy, almost black fruit, this variety starts bearing at an earlier age than most cherry varieties. Ripens late in this zone. Self-fertile variety, plus it is a good pollenizer for other cherries.

LAPINS. This sweet purplish-black cherry is a favorite of the commercial growers. It is a productive and easy-to-grow variety from Canada that is crack resistant and flavorful. Ripens early to midseason in this zone. Self-fertile.

KORDIA. This sweet variety is originally from Czechoslovakia, and it produces heavy crops of large, firm, sweet, very black fruit. It needs a pollenizer.

ROYAL ANNE (ALSO CALLED NAPOLEON). This is the sweet maraschino cherry variety and also is used for commercial canning. It is very consistent, productive, and hardy with lots of yellow fruit with a rose blush in

midseason. It requires another midseason bloomer as a pollenizer.

MONTMORENCY. This heirloom sour cherry produces abundant crops of large, bright to dark-red, mildly acidic fruit with clear juice for making delicious pies. It is a reliable, compact, productive, and disease-resistant tree. It's pretty too. Blooms in late spring. Self-fertile.

BEST BETS FOR ZONE 9A

LAPINS. This sweet purplish-black cherry is a favorite of the commercial growers. It is a productive and easy-to-grow variety from Canada that is crack resistant and flavorful. Self-fertile.

BING. The most famous cherry, the Bing, has large, firm garnet to black-red fruit with glossy, smooth skin. They are produced in abundance on a vigorous spreading tree. Great for fresh eating, cooking, or canning. Needs a pollenizer.

RAINIER. These sweet and tasty cherries have pretty yellow skin with a red blush and the flesh is clear to light yellow. There is often some discoloration on the skin that can indicate high sugar content. Needs a pollenizer.

MONTMORENCY. This heirloom sour cherry produces abundant crops of large, bright to dark-red, mildly acidic fruit with clear juice for making delicious pies. It is a reliable, compact, productive, and disease-resistant tree. It's pretty too. Blooms in late spring. Self-fertile.

ENGLISH MORELO. A late-ripening, somewhat tart cherry best used for pies and cooking, this almost black fruit with very dark-red juice is great for making brandies or preserves, canning, freezing, or drying. Trees are productive and self-fertile.

BEST BETS FOR ZONE 10

This zone is said to not be the best for cherries, as they are prone to a short lifespan, cankers, and bacterial oozes in this climate. That being said, many backyard gardeners in this zone are thrilled with their healthy, prolific, and long-lived cherry trees. Check with your neighbors.

BING. The most famous cherry, the Bing, has large, firm garnet to black-red fruit with glossy, smooth skin and is produced in abundance on a vigorous spreading tree. Great for fresh eating, cooking, or canning. Needs a pollenizer.

LAPINS. This sweet purplish-black cherry is a favorite of the commercial growers. It is a productive and easy-to-grow variety from Canada that is crack resistant and flavorful. Self-fertile.

MONTMORENCY. This heirloom sour cherry produces abundant crops of large, bright to dark-red, mildly acidic fruit with clear juice for making delicious pies. It is a reliable, compact, productive, and disease-resistant tree. It's pretty too. Blooms in late spring. Self-fertile.

PITTING CHERRIES

Now that you have your own cherry tree, you may want to buy a cherry pitter, although some people swear an old-fashioned hairpin works just as well. Whichever method you choose, be sure and wear an apron while popping out the stones. If cherry juice does splash on your white cotton tee, stretch the fabric over a bowl. From at least a foot above, pour boiling water over the unwashed cherry stain. Watch the red fade away.

THE GLORIOUS CHERRY HARVEST

Besides popping fresh cherries right into our mouths, cherry pie is the first thing a lot of us think of when we think cherry, or cherry crisp, but have you ever tried dipping cherries into a chocolate fondue? Freeze some of your harvest to enjoy throughout the winter. Place the seeded cherries in a single layer on a baking sheet and put them in the freezer. When frozen, you can put them in resealable plastic freezer bags for wintertime cherry cobbler or a myriad of other recipes. Cold cherry soup with yogurt sounds great, but how about pork tenderloin with cherry sauce, or cherry barbecue sauce, or a quesadilla with salty cheese and sour cherries? Brandied cherries are easy to make, although they need to age for a few months. Be sure to keep these away from the kids!

SOUR CHERRY CLAFOUTI

As their name suggests, sour cherries, unlike their sweet cousins, aren't the best choice for eating out of hand. Instead, bake them up in a sweet batter with a kiss of almond to make the best use of the sour cherry's considerable assets. Seattle chef Renee Erickson of The Walrus and the Carpenter serves this clafouti warm, dusted with confectioners' sugar and drizzled with heavy cream. If you have berry bushes tucked in your garden beside your tree, the same basic recipe works for blackberries, raspberries, huckleberries, and blueberries once cherry season has passed. MAKES ONE 9-INCH CLAFOUTI

2 large eggs, room temperature

½ cup plus 2 tablespoons sugar

Zest from half a lemon

1 teaspoon almond extract

6 ounces or ¾ cup half-and-half

6 tablespoons flour

1 cup pitted sour cherries

Preheat the oven to 375 degrees F. Grease and sugar a 9-inch pie pan, making sure the butter extends all the way up the sides to help the clafouti rise. Set aside.

In a medium-sized bowl, crack the eggs and whisk for 2 minutes, or until they are nice and fluffy. Add ½ cup of the sugar and lemon zest and whisk until the sugar dissolves. Mix together the almond extract, half-and-half, and flour; whisk to combine until all the flour has been incorporated.

Pour the batter into the pie pan and dot with the sour cherries. Sprinkle the top with the remaining sugar and place in oven. Bake for 30 to 40 minutes, or until the batter is brown and set and the edges are slightly puffed. Serve warm with confectioners' sugar and heavy cream.

WINTER CHICKEN WITH DRIED CHERRY STUFFING AND ARTICHOKES

A dish for those dark, cold winter days when the cherry blossoms seem very far off. Dried cherries add the lift in a sprightly dressing that brings out the best in an organic, free-range bird. If you're one of those who likes dressing as much as meat, Chef Lisa Scott Owens of The Mark Restaurant gives you permission to prepare extra stuffing, adding in seasonal veggies and roots like rutabaga or winter squash if you like. Coat with olive oil, rosemary, and garlic, and season with salt and pepper. Pile it all on a sheet pan and place in the oven to roast when the chicken is halfway done. MAKES 4 SERVINGS

1 whole organic free-range chicken

Kosher salt and cracked black pepper

Extra-virgin olive oil

1 cup quartered waxy potatoes, such as butter, fingerling, or red, scrubbed

½ cup dried cherries, soaked in warm water for 30 minutes, then drained

¼ cup walnuts

2 sprigs fresh rosemary, bruised

3 cloves garlic, peeled

4 small slices of lemon

2 artichokes, trimmed

6 tablespoons butter

Preheat the oven to 400 degrees F. Rinse the chicken, then dry it very well with a paper towel. Season the bird inside and out with salt and freshly cracked black pepper and rub with olive oil. In a mixing bowl, toss the potatoes, cherries, walnuts, rosemary, garlic, and lemon with olive oil to coat. Stuff the bird with the potato mixture and truss it, if you like. Put it on a well-oiled baking sheet or in a large oven-safe pan.

Brown the chicken for about 15 minutes, then reduce the heat to 350 degrees F. Depending on the size of the chicken, the cook time can be an hour and a half to two hours (you're looking for an internal temperature of 165 degrees F).

While the chicken is roasting, place the artichokes in a pot to steam for 45 minutes, or until a leaf comes out easily when pulled. Melt the butter in a small saucepan over low heat.

Remove chicken from the oven when done and allow to rest. Remove the twine if you trussed the bird. Remove the roasted vegetable stuffing to a bowl and season to taste with salt and freshly cracked pepper. Place the stuffing on the platter with the chicken. Cut the stem ends off the artichokes and serve with melted butter for dipping.

ROASTED BLACK CHERRIES WITH TAHITIAN VANILLA ICE CREAM

Though well-known for his chocolate creations, chocolatier-pâtissier extraordinaire Thierry Busset of Vancouver, B.C.'s Thierry also recognizes that a perfectly fresh cherry is a wonder in and of itself. This easy-to-execute recipe intensifies the fruit's flavor by pan-roasting, then brightens both taste and color with a hit of raspberry. Serving with homemade vanilla ice cream would be a nice touch. MAKES 4 SERVINGS

Recipe Note: See the recipe for Vanilla Ice Cream in chapter 7, at the recipe for "Marsala–Roasted Fig with Almond Custard, Vanilla Ice Cream, and Oat Tuile."

8 ounces raspberries, fresh or frozen

⅓ cup granulated sugar

¼ cup high-quality extra-virgin olive oil

2¼ pounds fresh cherries, stemmed, pitted, and halved

Cherry liqueur (optional)

Vanilla ice cream

Make a coulis by blending the raspberries and sugar in a food processor. Pass the mixture through a fine-mesh sieve to remove the seeds. Set aside.

Preheat a frying pan over medium heat, but don't allow the pan to get hot enough for the olive oil to smoke. Add the olive oil, then tip in the cherries. Flip the pan two or three times to make sure the cherries are coated with olive oil. Cook for about 2 minutes, until the cherries are just warm throughout. If using cherry liqueur, deglaze the pan with a few splashes of it.

Pour the cherries from the pan into a bowl. Replace the pan over the flame and pour in the raspberry coulis. Bring the coulis to boil and reduce for approximately 3 minutes. Add the cherries to the reduced coulis and flip two or three times until the cherries are thoroughly coated.

To serve, use a slotted spoon to divide the cherries among four bowls, spooning the desired amount of coulis on top. Finish with a scoop of vanilla ice cream.

FRESH CHERRY AND ALMOND CUSTARD PARFAITS WITH EASY ALMOND BRITTLE

Something about warming fresh cherries makes them taste more plump and delicious. In this recipe by Portland's Ivy Manning, warm, ripe cherries are made all the more sexy by sandwiching them between layers of silky almond cream and sugared almond brittle. Most of the recipe can be prepared in advance and put together at the last minute. **MAKES 4 SERVINGS**

ALMOND BRITTLE

1 egg white

1 cup sliced almonds

¼ cup sugar

ALMOND CUSTARD

3 egg yolks

¼ cup sugar

¼ cup all-purpose flour

1 cup whole milk

1 tablespoon amaretto liqueur, or ½ teaspoon almond extract

1 tablespoon unsalted butter

CHERRY SAUCE

3 cups pitted Bing cherries

3 tablespoons sugar

2 tablespoons amaretto liqueur

Preheat the oven to 350 degrees F. Line a small, rimmed baking sheet with parchment paper and spray with nonstick cooking spray.

For the BRITTLE, whisk the egg white in a small bowl until frothy, then discard half of the egg white. Add the almonds and sugar and toss with a fork to combine. Spread the almond mixture on the baking sheet and place in the oven. Bake, stirring occasionally, until the almonds are golden brown and crisp, about 10 minutes. The brittle can be made up to one week ahead and kept in an airtight container.

For the ALMOND CUSTARD, whisk the egg yolks and sugar in a medium mixing bowl until thick and pale yellow. Fold in the flour and stir until combined. Put the milk in a small saucepan over medium heat and bring to a simmer. Gradually whisk the hot milk into the egg and sugar mixture.

Pour the mixture back into the saucepan and cook over medium heat, whisking constantly, until bubbly and thickened, about 2 minutes. Strain the sauce into a medium bowl, whisk in the amaretto and butter and allow the custard to cool to room temperature, stirring occasionally. Place plastic wrap directly on the surface of the custard and refrigerate until cold. (The custard can be made up to three days ahead, whisk to smooth.)

For the CHERRY SAUCE, place the cherries and sugar in a sauté pan. Bring to a simmer over medium heat and cook, stirring frequently, until the cherries release their juice and the sugar is dissolved, about 10 minutes. Take the pan off heat and stir in the amaretto.

To assemble the parfait, layer the warm cherries and cooled custard in large wine glasses or parfait glasses. Top with shards of the almond brittle.

12

Quince

(Cydonia oblonga)

The once-popular quince has been an underappreciated backyard fruit tree in the past few decades except for those few gardeners who upheld the tradition of cooking the fruit into splendid jams and jellies. However, this fruit is making a well-deserved comeback and has been increasingly featured in restaurant fare and cookbooks in the past few years. The pretty trees have large but delicate-looking cup-shaped white flowers with a pink blush in the spring and bright to pale-green, slightly fuzzy leaves.

The quince is closely related to a pear or apple tree, but it is smaller and more bushlike. The fruit varies greatly by variety. Quince can be apple- or pear-shaped and four to six inches long. The fruit of the old standard variety is astringent and always needs to be cooked to be edible, and even then it is usually only eaten after some amount of sugar has been added. Quince contains relatively high levels of pectin, a thickener, which is why it is so often made into jellies or added to help thicken jelly made of other fruit.

The common quince trees seem to thrive on neglect, steadily growing along on long-abandoned homesteads, but they don't mind a little care if you have the time. They appreciate regular water, but skip the fertilizer as it promotes vigorous growth that could invite fire blight to which they are susceptible (although it is not a huge problem in the Pacific maritime regions). This is one of those amazing fruit trees that don't seem to be fazed by the summer fog that occasionally blankets the coast. They actually prefer heavy clay soils because their roots are shallow. The gnarled branches and trunk of the quince often develop black knots, but thankfully this doesn't signal disease and can be appreciated as a novel, healthy feature of the tree.

Not much pruning is necessary except for controlling suckers at the base of the trees. Cut back to keep the foliage full, as branches tend to droop and trees can easily become leggy. They are frequently trained as bushes, but even full-grown trees rarely exceed fifteen feet without ever having been touched by pruning shears. Fruit doesn't need thinning unless a branch looks in danger of breaking under the weight.

In the fall the fruit turns a golden yellow and the arresting fragrance is noticeable when just walking near the tree. The tantalizing aroma is both familiar and exotic—imagine a pear rolled in citrus juice and tropical flower petals. That aroma indicates harvest time. Don't wait for the fruit to soften because it won't, yet it bruises easily and needs to be handled carefully. It has a fuzzy covering that rubs off easily. Be careful of your fingers when cutting into a quince. Most varieties are as hard as an acorn squash. The flesh turns from white to shades of pink and red as it cooks.

As unique varieties have come to the United States from Russia and Central Asia, more uses for the lowly quince are being appreciated. The new varieties retain the good qualities of the standard or common quince but produce fruit that gets sweet enough to be eaten fresh. After harvest the fruit of these imported varieties softens to a pear-like texture. After harvesting your quinces, leave them out in a bowl or set them out on a windowsill for two to three weeks so you can enjoy their shape and color as well as their smell. If you want to keep them longer, refrigerate them for another month or two in a sealed plastic bag with a towel to absorb any moisture.

Best Bets for Quince

The following lists tell which quince varieties are suited to their respective zones. There could be more that would grow well in each zone; however, these varieties are the ones that experts most highly recommend.

BEST BETS FOR ZONE 8B

Most quinces are grown as bushes in this zone.

PINEAPPLE. This is the variety that was developed by Luther Burbank in the 1890s and has been the most commercially available of the quinces. The flavor is reminiscent of pineapple, although the quince is tart. The tree is cold hardy but has low chill requirements, so it is a great bet for all of the Pacific maritime regions. It bears heavy crops of large fruit to use in cooking. Self-fertile.

AROMATNAYA. A new variety from Russia that is sweet enough to eat fresh, this quince tree bears an abundant crop of round, yellow fruit that smells like citrus and ripens in October. Leave it on a windowsill until it begins to soften and slice it thinly to eat—excellent for cooking too. This quince is even more disease resistant than other quince varieties. Self-fertile.

KARP'S SWEET QUINCE. This variety was brought to the United States from southern Peru and named after fruit connoisseur and writer David Karp. When it is grown in the Pacific Northwest, the tree doesn't produce fruit as sweet as that grown in hotter regions, but it is less astringent and woody than standard quinces. Self-fertile.

BEST BETS FOR ZONE 8A

AROMATNAYA. A new variety from Russia that is sweet enough to eat fresh, this tree bears an abundant crop of round, yellow fruit that smells like citrus and ripens in October. Leave it on a windowsill until it begins to soften and slice it thinly to eat—excellent for cooking too. This quince is even more disease resistant than other quince varieties. Self-fertile.

KAUNCHING. This mellow, tender variety comes from Central Asia. It is medium-sized and very sweet and flavorful. You can sprinkle it with sugar and eat it out of hand, make delicious preserves, or cook with it. Self-fertile.

KUGANSKAYA. A pretty, easy-to-grow small tree, the Kuganskaya bears a large crop of round, bright-yellow fruit that is more tender than most quince. Eat it fresh or use it for cooking or preserves. Self-fertile.

BEST BETS FOR ZONE 9B

ORANGE. An heirloom variety with light-orange flesh, this quince is delicious, and each round fruit can each weigh more than a pound. Cold hardy and very productive. Self-fertile.

SMYRNA. The easy-to-grow tree is productive, reliable, and vigorous. It has large, yellow pear-shaped fruit with great aroma and mild tasty flavor that is delicious for cooking and making desserts, preserves, and jellies. Self-fertile.

AROMATANYA. A new variety from Russia is sweet enough to eat fresh, this tree bears an abundant crop of round, yellow fruit that smells like citrus and ripens in October. Leave it on a windowsill until it begins to soften and slice it thinly to eat—excellent for cooking too. This quince is even more disease resistant than other quince varieties. Self-fertile.

BEST BETS FOR ZONE 9A

SMYRNA. The easy-to-grow tree is productive, reliable, and vigorous. It has large, yellow pear-shaped fruit with great aroma and mild tasty flavor that is delicious for cooking and making desserts, preserves, and jellies. Self-fertile.

PINEAPPLE. This variety has been the most commercially available of the quinces. The flavor is reminiscent of pineapple, although the quince is tart. The tree is cold-hardy but has low chill requirements, so it is a great bet for all of our regions. It bears heavy crops of large fruit to use in cooking. Self-fertile.

BEST BETS FOR ZONE 10

PINEAPPLE. This variety has been the most commercially available of the quinces. The flavor is reminiscent of pineapple, although the quince is tart. The tree is cold-hardy but has low chill requirements, so it is a great bet for all of our regions. It bears heavy crops of large fruit to use in cooking. Self-fertile.

SMYRNA. The easy-to-grow tree is productive, reliable, and vigorous. It has large, yellow pear-shaped fruit with great aroma and mild tasty flavor that is delicious for cooking and making desserts, preserves, and jellies. Self-fertile.

THE GLORIOUS QUINCE HARVEST

The color of quince jam or jelly is beautiful enough just sitting on the shelf in a clear jar to justify any effort expended in making it, but it's the taste that will keep you preserving your quinces every year. The quince is sometimes used in place of apple in cooking, but unlike apple, quince holds its form and texture when cooked. Quince is prized in many countries for its flavor in dishes both sweet and savory. Try using quince in a compote for pork tenderloin or a Moroccan tagine. Dice quince and cook it with currants and a few cranberries instead of the traditional cranberry sauce at Thanksgiving. Membrillo (the Spanish word for quince) or Dulce de Membrillo refers to a quince jam that is firm enough to be formed into blocks and is popular in Spain, Portugal, and many South American countries, where it is savored with aged Manchego cheese for a dessert or served spread on toast for breakfast.

MOSTARDA DI VENEZIA

Chef Cathy Whims of Portland's Nostrana reports that she first tasted this mostarda—a quince and mustard preserve—some years ago while studying in Venice with noted Italian culinary experts Marcella and Victor Hazan. Every October, a little cheese shop in the Rialto market sells this seasonal preserve. The mostarda that follows is Whims's adaptation of a recipe from Anna del Conte. Chef Whims thinks this mostarda tastes best after three weeks, but at the restaurant they have used it the next day to good effect. Even if you can't make it to Venice, cook up a batch of "Mostarda di Venezia" with your own backyard quince and dream of Italy. MAKES 3½ PINTS

4 pounds ripe quince, scrubbed, peeled, cored, and coarsely chopped
3 cups white wine, preferably Tocai Friulano
Grated peel and juice of two lemons
Sugar, as needed
⅓ cup dry mustard powder
1 cup candied orange peel, diced
Salt

Place the quince in a heavy-bottomed saucepan and cover with white wine, lemon juice, and lemon peel. Bring to a boil over high heat, reduce to simmer and cook until soft, adding small amounts of water if the wine evaporates.

Purée mixture through a food mill. Weigh the resulting mixture and add an equal weight of sugar. Return to the saucepan.

In a small bowl, make a slurry with the dry mustard powder and a little hot water. Pour the slurry into the saucepan with the candied orange peel and season to taste with salt. Bring the mixture back to a simmer and cook until thick, about 30 minutes. Cool and refrigerate in an airtight container.

DUTCH BABY WITH CARAMELIZED SPICED QUINCE

This dish exemplifies the exquisite result of blending alpine flavors and Pacific Northwest foods, the hallmark of Chef Chris Israel's Grüner Restaurant in Portland, Oregon. Terrific for breakfast or even for an unusual (and delicious) dessert, this recipe addresses the lovely quince's need for cooking by poaching the fruit in an aromatic syrup scented with citrus and clove. This means you can easily prepare the quince the night before, then quickly sauté the fruit and pop the pancake in the oven. You'll have breakfast ready before the coffee is done. **MAKES 4 SERVINGS**

POACHED QUINCE

2 cups sugar

2 cups water

2 cloves

2 strips lemon zest (removed with a vegetable peeler)

1 cinnamon stick

2 ripe quince, scrubbed, peeled, cored, and quartered

DUTCH BABY

2 eggs

3 ounces whole milk

⅓ cup all-purpose flour

Generous pinch of salt

1 tablespoon sugar, plus 1 teaspoon sugar

1 tablespoon butter

2 poached quince quarters (recipe above), each cut into 5 to 6 lengthwise slices

Confectioners' sugar, for dusting

Make a simple syrup by combining the sugar and water in a medium saucepan. Stir in the cloves, lemon zest, and half of the cinnamon stick. Bring the mixture to a boil over medium heat, then reduce to a simmer.

Add the QUINCE to the mixture and simmer until soft and darkened in color, about 15 to 30 minutes. Remove from heat and let cool. Store quince refrigerated in syrup.

For the DUTCH BABY, preheat the oven to 450 degrees F. In a blender, combine the eggs, milk, flour, salt, and 1 tablespoon of the sugar and mix on high until well blended, about 20 to 30 seconds.

In an ovenproof sauté pan or cast-iron pan, melt the butter and the rest of the sugar over medium heat. Add the poached quince and cook and stir until golden brown. Turn the pieces and cook to caramelize the other side. Pour in the batter and cook on top of stove for a few seconds, then transfer the mixture to the preheated oven. Bake for 7 minutes, or until puffed and just golden.

Turn the pancake out of the sauté pan and fold in half if you wish. Dust with plenty of confectioners' sugar and drizzle with the quince poaching liquid if desired, or even a little maple syrup. Enjoy.

APPLE-QUINCE BUTTER

Cookbook author and Seattle Go Go Green gardener Amy Pennington prefers to use heirloom apples for this luscious butter that hails from her book Urban Pantry. *She prefers Winesap, but Macintosh, Spitzenburg, Rome, or Empire will do as well. Fruit butters sit on low heat for a very long time before thickening, so make sure to allot a few hours for this one. Pennington likes to smear a layer of fruit butter on puff pastry, cover with thinly sliced apples, sprinkle with Demerara sugar, and bake for an easy dessert or use to line the base of a tart.* **MAKES ABOUT 5 HALF-PINTS**

2 cups water

4 cups organic apple cider

2 pounds quince, scrubbed, peeled, and chopped into 1-inch pieces

2 pounds apples, scrubbed, peeled, and chopped into 1-inch pieces (include core and seeds)

2 cups sugar

1 lemon, squeezed of juice and halves reserved

1 teaspoon freshly grated cinnamon

½ teaspoon freshly ground cloves

½ teaspoon freshly ground nutmeg

In large stockpot, add the water, apple cider, quince, and apples. The liquid in the pot should just cover the fruit. If there is not enough liquid, add more apple cider or water to cover. Place over medium to medium-high heat and bring to a simmer. Cook until all the fruit is soft and you can mash it with the back of a spoon.

Working in batches, add the fruit to a blender (only half full at a time, as hot liquids expand) and purée. (You may also use a food mill, if you prefer.) When all the fruit is puréed, put it back into the stockpot. Stir in the sugar, lemon juice, cinnamon, cloves, and nutmeg and return to medium heat.

Apple butter takes a long while to thicken. Keep your pot over medium to medium-low heat, stirring continuously every few minutes, taking care not to let it burn. If the fruit butter is too hot and sticking to the bottom of your pot, turn the heat down. The apple–quince butter is done when a small spoonful is placed on a plate and no liquid separates out, creating a ring around the fruit butter. Cooking time can take anywhere from 1 to 2 hours.

Pour the thick apple–quince butter into jars; gently tap the bottom of the jars on a counter to release any air bubbles. Seal using proper canning methods, or store in your refrigerator.

13

Lesser Known
Fruit Trees

The trees in this section thrive in some maritime zones, but they don't grow or barely hang on in others. Some of them are subtropical and need the relative warmth of the southern or more inland regions; others need significant chilling hours and are fruitful in the cooler zones.

Medlar *(Mespilus germanica)*

The medlar has been a popular dessert fruit in Europe for hundreds of years. A beautiful little deciduous tree, it is a relative of apple, pear, and hawthorn and usually only grows to eight to ten feet. It can bear fruit in as little as two years. It has large but delicate white flowers at the tips of the branches in spring, which grow into chestnut-brown fruit with an open bottom and a calyx "crown" that somewhat resembles a jaunty court jester's cap. A medlar is usually grown on pear or quince rootstock. Unlike planting most other fruit trees, the Home Orchard Society recommends planting the medlar with the graft union below the soil line so that both the rootstock and medlar roots can grow and provide support for the tree. Lightly prune to keep the center open.

The fruit is picked when it is hard and then it has to *blet*—a word that comes from French and means to overripen, to *seriously* overripen. Keep the medlars at room temperature until they are mushy. If you eat one before it is very soft, it will be astringent just like an unripe Hachiya persimmon. As the medlar blets (don't you love that word?), the fruit becomes rich, spicy, and soft and develops the taste and feel of fruit butter with a cinnamon-applesauce flavor. Now you can put a hole in the skin and suck out the flesh and the rounded seeds.

BEST BETS FOR MEDLAR

The medlar will grow in all of our zones, but even though it should grow in zone 10, it is happier with a little more winter chill than Zone 10 usually provides. Medlars aren't bothered by pests or disease, and they are self-fertile.

MARRON. This naturally small tree will grow six to eight feet, bloom at the tips of branches, and produce abundant crops of very tasty, chestnut-colored fruits. Self-fertile.

BREDA GIANT. From Holland, this productive variety will give you a large harvest of sweet and fine-textured spicy, 1½ to 1¾-inch fruit. Self-fertile.

THE GLORIOUS MEDLAR HARVEST

The taste is either loved or hated—there is little middle ground with a medlar. After it has softened, it can be eaten out of hand or made into preserves. Mix chilled medlar pulp gently into whipped cream and some sugar for a mousse-like dessert, or use it like pumpkin in pie making. It is a good accompaniment for dessert wines.

Jujube *(Ziziphus jujuba)*

The first thing many of us think of when we hear the word "jujube" is the big box of brightly colored candies at a theater's snack bar. The jujube fruit you can grow in your yard is sweet and sometimes round, but that's about as far as the likeness goes, and eating a small bag of homegrown jujube fruits at the movies would be a much healthier option.

The jujube is native to China and is sometimes called Chinese Date. The deciduous tree, with its often contorted and sometimes thorny branches, can grow twenty to thirty feet. This is not a fussy tree. Let it grow or prune it to stay short enough to reach the fruit. Pruning is not needed to improve fruit production. Fertilize it, or not. It's fairly drought resistant, but it does require a well-drained soil and, not to be picky, actually prefers soil on the sandy side. The jujube is not bothered by any of the pests or diseases found in North America. It buds in late spring after danger of frost has passed. It can withstand high heat in the summers and cold in the winters, but the actual chill hours it requires are low. These attributes (well, except for the thorns) make this tree a great pick for all of the Pacific maritime zones, as long as you have a spot in your yard with enough sun to ripen the fruit.

You won't notice the modest but profuse yellow flowers on the jujube unless you are close to the tree, but the bees love the flowers and have no trouble finding them. The crisp fruit tastes like a sweet apple and is usually the size of a small plum. The jujube flowers over several weeks, and the fruits also don't ripen all at once, so you will not be inundated with a deluge of fruit. They can be stored at room temperature for about a week or in the refrigerator for long periods.

BEST BETS FOR JUJUBE

These are the most widely grown varieties:

LI . This variety will produce an abundant crop of large mahogany-brown flavorful fruit with a tiny seed. Crisp and flavorful, this jujube is oval. Self-fertile, but plant two varieties to get more fruit.

LANG. This pretty tree bears fruit that looks like a small pear that tastes best if it is left to ripen fully on the tree. If your summer has been cool, you can pick the fruit when it is still half green and let it finish ripening on your counter. It needs another jujube for best pollination.

THE GLORIOUS JUJUBE HARVEST

Besides eating as many as you can as soon as they ripen, you can eat jujube cooked in sauces, jams, compotes, or cakes. They are often dried and used in place of dates or raisins. Jujube can be dried slowly in an oven or dehydrator or—and this is unusual—they can be left on the tree to dry if the weather is dry, before picking and storing in airtight containers.

Mulberry *(Morus)*

"Here We Go Round the Mulberry Bush" and "Pop Goes the Weasel"—this tree could have you humming childhood tunes. It is easy to see how a Weeping Mulberry would be a child's favorite outdoor spot too, as it can look like a blanket draped over a big umbrella. A Weeping Mulberry grows straight up six to eight feet in height, and the branches grow outward and then down with leaves often trailing the ground. Remove the lower branches inside the "tent" to leave a wide-open space around the trunk. Who could resist climbing in? What a great place for hide-and-seek, a summer picnic or tea party, or just a place to get away from it all with a book.

In colonial times varieties of large mulberry trees were brought to the United States from China to feed silkworms. The fledgling U.S. silk business was not competitive, so it died out and mulberry trees were left to fend for themselves. They did a good job of it over most of North America, growing and hybridizing with the native red mulberry. After the silk spinning industry declined, mulberry trees were cultivated for their fruit, but because they are difficult to pick and delicate to ship, or even get to a nearby market, the call for them dwindled also.

Despite their name and resemblance to blackberries, mulberries are fruits, not berries. Mulberry trees are prized as shade trees. Some of them can make some big shade too, since they can grow to be sixty feet tall, although many of the trees sold in the West are small varieties, including the Weeping Mulberry and the Illinois Everbearing. Female trees bear fruit whose staining power is legendary. Don't plant a mulberry near a house or driveway if you don't want a tie-dyed effect, but do plant it in the sun if you want sweet fruit. Black mulberries have the best sweet-tart taste and, as a smaller variety, can be planted in containers if you don't want them in the ground.

BEST BETS FOR MULBERRY

Mulberries will grow in all of our zones. They are reputed to do better in Oregon and California than in Washington, but that being said, many Washingtonians are enjoying the fruits of their trees.

ILLINOIS EVERBEARING. One of the best trees for many regions of North America, including California and the Pacific Northwest, the Illinois Everbearing has tasty, 1½-inch-long fruit. Very hardy, it grows slowly to fifteen feet, and the fruit can be harvested all summer long. Resistant to pests and diseases. Self-fertile.

WEEPING MULBERRY. Jet-black small, sweet fruit is borne on this six- to eight-foot tree with drooping branch structure that is happy in the ground or in a pot. Pest and disease resistant. Self-fertile.

THE GLORIOUS MULBERRY HARVEST

Mulberries don't ripen all at once, so you can be harvesting over a longer time than with many fruits. Most people just stand at their trees and graze and say that few of the berries ever make it to the house, but if you have a large tree or more than one, mulberries have many uses in the kitchen. Cobblers, pies, tarts, and fruit leathers are wonderful made with mulberries as are wines and cordials and dried raisinlike treats.

Feijoa or Pineapple Guava
(*Feijoa sellowiana* or
Acca sellowiana)

On hearing "guava," most people in our corner of the world think of the Pineapple Guava, which is not a true guava. Recently, people have begun to call the fruit and tree Feijoa instead of Pineapple Guava. The bluish-green bush or small tree is evergreen and attractive even without fruit. Several Feijoas planted in a row make a nice hedge. Prune them to whatever shape you want or allow them to grow naturally to twenty feet. Feijoas can take several years to start producing fruit. Brushing the flowers with your hand or a soft brush will help with pollination. The flowers are a beautiful crimson-red color with pink petals and long bright-red stamens tipped with bright-yellow pollen. When the petals are soft, they become mildly sweet, with some of the Feijoa taste and can be used in fruit salads or on top of a dessert.

If the weather is warm enough and your tree is in full sun, the flowers will develop into green oval fruits five to seven months later. You might imagine you feel the warm breezes of Hawaii when you smell or taste a Feijoa. The flavor ranges from slightly tart to very sweet. Some say it is a melding of banana and pineapple, while others claim they also taste hints of strawberry, lemon, passion fruit, and guava. Lots of edible seeds inside add another pleasing flavor. Most people cut the fruit in half and scoop out the pulp with a spoon.

The Feijoa fruit can be picked before fully ripe and left out on the counter for a few days, but the flavor and texture are best if they are left on the tree till they are ready to drop. Gently squeeze the fruit. If it is ready to pick, it will give slightly. Pick up dropped fruit daily so it doesn't become overripe, and eat it soon as it will only keep a few days when fully ripe.

BEST BETS FOR FEIJOA
. . . .

Feijoa varieties grow well in all zones, but in Zone 8b you will probably have to be content to enjoy the flowers. In other zones you could be harvesting fruit in the late fall or winter if you provide your Feijoa with at least six hours of sun.

COOLIDGE. A good variety for the Northwest, the Coolidge bears a profuse crop of pear-shaped fruit with crinkly skin. Pest resistant and self-fertile.

MAMMOTH. By the name of this variety you would expect large fruit, and you wouldn't be disappointed. The round-to-oval fruit with slightly wrinkled skin can weigh more than eight ounces. It ripens early and has great flavor with a slightly gritty flesh. Bears larger fruit with another tree for pollination.

ROBERT. This variety from New Zealand has beautiful flowers and flavorful but sometimes gritty fruit on a naturally small tree that does well in containers. Self-fertile.

THE GLORIOUS
FEIJOA HARVEST

If there are any left after you have eaten your fill right from the tree, chop up some feijoas and add them to muffins or make a feijoa crisp. Use them to make smoothies, jam, chutney, salsa, or substitute feijoa for apples in making cake. Add puréed feijoa to sweeten yogurt, or mix them into savory dishes like curried chicken, or roast them with pork. Feijoa wine and cider are popular in New Zealand.

Loquat (*Eriobotrya japonica*)

You'd be hard pressed to find loquats in grocery stores because of their delicate skin, but aficionados contend that this fruit deserves to be upgraded in popularity. If you don't live within walking distance of a loquat tree, it's possible you have never tasted a fresh one. There is disagreement on just how to describe the taste of a loquat—apricot and guava; plum, apricot, and pineapple; cantaloupe and passion fruit, and the list goes on. Maybe it is enough to say that loquat has a mild but exotic apricotlike flavor. A sun-warmed loquat straight off the tree is a springtime pleasure. It is strange, then, that in many areas the evergreen loquat trees with their large, pointed, dark-green leaves are grown for their ornamental and shade-giving qualities and the fruit is often left to the birds or

to drop to the ground. Maybe some people are put off by the two to five large seeds, but for those who know and love a loquat, eating around the seeds is a small price to pay for the luscious taste.

Loquats are common street and yard trees in the coastal regions of Central and Northern California. Several varieties prefer the humidity and cooler weather those regions offer, although trees in very foggy areas might not get enough of the heat they need to set or ripen fruit.

Originally from China, loquat trees bloom in the fall or winter and fruit is ready to eat in very early spring. Loquat trees are the souls of tolerance. They are tolerant of soil types as long as they have good drainage. They are tolerant of wind. Partial shade is tolerated, although they prefer sun all day. They will attractively tolerate being espaliered or even grown in large containers, though they would rather grow ten to twenty feet. They will even tolerate some drought. A loquat tree is utterly tolerant of indifference but doesn't mind a little pampering now and then. If you reward their forbearance with some good compost or balanced fertilizer in midwinter, they will repay you tastefully when the fruit comes in.

Pests are few, especially if you don't count the deer that like to nibble the leaves or the birds that are happy to help you consume your tree-ripened crop. You will get a better yearly crop if you clip off some of the young fruit in each cluster. Prune loquat trees just after harvest for size or let them grow as they will. Choose your variety well, as some loquats need more heat than others. Usually the white-fleshed varieties are best for coastal areas. Eat them right off the tree, cook with them, or dry them quickly because these treats don't last. In the refrigerator or a cool place, loquats will possibly be good for up to a week.

BEST BETS FOR LOQUATS

Loquat trees grow beautifully in all of the Pacific coastal zones, but it is rare to get fruit in Zones 8b and 8a. In Zones 9b, 9a, and 10, try one of these varieties:

GOLD NUGGET. This sweet loquat with deep-orange flesh and slightly apricotlike aroma grows well in the maritime climate. Said to be the best loquat in Zone 10. Self-fertile.

CHAMPAGNE. This yellow-skinned variety has fragrant flowers in the fall and white-fleshed tart and juicy fruit of very good quality. Self-fertile.

MCBETH. The McBeth has tasty, very large, round, yellow-skinned fruit with firm but juicy cream-white flesh. Thin fruits for size and quality of the fruit but also to prevent branches breaking from too much weight. Self-fertile.

BIG JIM. A large teardrop-shaped fruit with orange skin and orange flesh, the Big Jim is juicy and flavorful, tasting somewhat like a mild but slightly tangy peach. Self-fertile.

THE GLORIOUS LOQUAT HARVEST

Most loquats are eaten right off the tree. Kids especially like them. They are high in pectin, so making jellies, jams, marmalades, and chutneys is especially easy. Simmer puréed loquats with sugar, water, and lemon zest until thick, then spread it on toast or muffins. Loquats are a refreshing addition to fruit salads or cobblers, and delectable poached in light syrup.

Conclusion:
The Sad Tale of the Avocado

Wouldn't we all like to grow an avocado tree or two? How wonderful would it be to step outside to pick a couple of perfectly ripe avocados for guacamole for dinner? The sad tale is that few of us will be able to grow an avocado tree that will bear fruit unless we live at the southeastern edges of the marine influence. Success in getting homegrown fruit from your tree to your table comes from knowing what you can nurture and grow in your environment and accepting and embracing the limits and opportunities of your climate.

Many of the fruits that will flourish in your yard will rarely be seen in grocery stores, but they will satisfy you in many more ways than just your taste buds. Food gardening can be an antidote to our out-of-balance world. Tending to the rhythm of fruit trees can soothe our souls—and ultimately put smiles on the faces of our families and friends.

Nature can be very forgiving. You don't have to do everything exactly the "right" way to get wonderful harvests from your trees. The key is to match the tree and the variety to the correct location. After that, if you follow a few basic guidelines and treat your trees in a manner somewhere between hovering micromanagement and outright neglect, your chances of success are excellent. Plant in the sun, provide the water they need when they are young, prune, and send them messages of thanks for their gifts to you.

Glossary

ALTERNATE BEARING. The alternating of heavy fruit production on a tree one year followed by light production the next year.

ANTHER. The pollen-bearing part of a flower.

BARE-ROOT TREE. A young tree dug out of the ground during the dormant season and shipped and sold with no dirt around the roots.

BENEFICIALS. Organisms that feed on or parasitize plant pests.

BERM. A mound or wall of earth often built around a young tree to help with irrigation.

BREBA CROP. The first of two crops produced by a fig tree each year that develop in the fall and ripen the next summer.

BUD. A small protuberance on a stem that may develop into a flower, leaf, or shoot.

CALIPER. In this context, the measurement of the diameter of a tree trunk or branch.

CALYX. The usually green outermost whorl of sepals of a flower collectively forming the outer layer of the developing bud.

CAMBIUM LAYER. The thin, actively dividing layer of cells between the bark and the wood that causes the stem to grow in diameter. When grafting, the cambium layers or at least a portion of the cambium layers of the two sections of wood must be in contact for them to grow together.

CANKER. A sunken or swollen section of decayed or diseased tissue on tree bark.

CENTRAL LEADER. A system of training a fruit tree often used for apples and pears, in which the main trunk grows vertically in the center of the tree with branches growing laterally around it.

CHILLING HOURS (OR CHILLING UNITS). The number of hours of temperature between 32 and 45 degrees Fahrenheit that accumulate in the winter.

CHILLING REQUIREMENT. How many cumulative hours may be required by a fruit tree in order to break dormancy and provide good growth and fruit production.

CLIMATE. The average course of the weather at a place over a period of years based on such factors as temperature, wind, and rain.

COLLAR. The slightly enlarged woody tissue around the base of a branch where it attaches to the trunk or another branch.

CROTCH. The angle formed where the trunk joins a main branch or between two branches.

CULTIVAR. From "cultivated variety." In common usage, "cultivar" and "variety" are used synonymously.

DECIDUOUS. Plants that drop their leaves at the end of the growing season.

DORMANT. A state of resting and not actively growing but protected from the environment.

DORMANT PRUNING. Pruning during dormant season invigorates growth the following spring.

DORMANT SEASON. The period in late fall, from just before the leaves drop, through the enlargement of buds just before growth starts (bud swell).

DRIP IRRIGATION. A low-volume watering system using tubing and drip emitters.

DRIP LINE. An imaginary line on the soil below the outermost branch tips around a tree.

DWARFING ROOTSTOCK. Rootstock that can produce a smaller and less vigorous tree.

ESPALIER. A system of tree training to grow trees in two planes, usually against a wall or fence or trained on horizontal wires.

FERTILIZATION. The process of pollination when the pollen joins with the ovules and a seed begins to grow *or* the application of nutrients to the soil or the tree.

FERTILIZER. A nutrient applied to the soil or the tree's leaves to provide nutrients.

FOOTIE. A disposable nylon stocking that some fruit tree growers put over each individual fruit to help protect it from insects as it grows.

FREESTONE. When the pit does not stick (or cling) to the flesh of the ripened fruit, such as a peach.

FUNGUS. An organism such as mold or mildew that lacks chlorophyll and reproduces through spores.

GENETIC OR NATURAL DWARF. A tree that stays small even if grafted onto a standard rootstock.

GIRDLE. Damage to a ring of bark tissue that encircles the trunk, branch, or root and interrupts the flow of water and nutrients.

GRAFTING. The process of joining a portion of one plant to another so they will grow as a single unit.

GRAFT UNION. The place on a trunk or branch that marks where the trunk was joined to the rootstock or where one branch was joined to another branch.

HEADING CUT. A pruning cut that takes a branch back to a bud but not all the way back to the point of the branch's origin.

JUNE DROP. A natural tendency for trees to shed some of their excess fruit. This does not always happen in the month of June but usually sometime within four weeks after bloom.

LARVA (PL. LARVAE). An immature form of an insect's development. Caterpillars of moths, the maggots of flies, and the grubs of beetles are all examples of larvae.

LATERAL BRANCH. A branch that grows outward from a scaffold branch or trunk but is not itself a scaffold branch.

LATERAL BUD. A bud on the side of a shoot or branch.

LEADER. A most vigorous upward-growing branch that becomes the main trunk in a tree trained to a central leader shape.

LEAF AXIL. The upper angle of the leaf stem where it attaches to the stem or shoot from which it grows.

LIMB. A large or main branch of a tree.

MAGGOT. The legless wormlike larva of various flies.

MICROCLIMATE. A local variation of climate that differs from the surrounding climate and is caused by many factors, which may include elevation, proximity to structures or bodies of water, sun exposure, fog patterns, and many other conditions. A microclimate may be a few square feet or many square miles.

MULCH. A layer of usually organic material, such as compost or wood chips, placed on the soil surface to conserve moisture, prevent weed growth, and prevent erosion.

MUMMY. A fruit that dries and shrivels yet remains hanging on the tree.

NODE. The point on a branch where the leaf is attached.

OPEN CENTER OR VASE PRUNING SYSTEM. A method of training a tree where the three to five scaffolding branches are developed low on the trunk with no central trunk.

ORGANIC. In the context of fruit, "organic" refers to crops grown without synthetic fertilizers, pesticides, or fungicides.

POLLEN. A mass of tiny, granular male cells formed in the anther of a flower's stamen that usually look like fine dust.

POLLENIZER (OR POLLINIZER). A plant that is the source of pollen. In fruit trees a pollenizer is the variety used as the pollen source for cross-pollination.

POLLINATION. The transfer of pollen from the anther to the stigma of either the same flower or from one flower to another.

POLLINATOR. The vector (usually a bee) that spreads the pollen from anther to stigma.

POME. A fruit with an outer thickened fleshy layer with a central core with usually five seeds enclosed in a capsule, like an apple or a pear.

RESISTANT VARIETY. A variety of a plant that is able to tolerate conditions that are harmful to other species or other varieties of the same species.

ROOTBOUND. A plant grown in a container that has roots which are tangled, matted, and grow around the edges of the container is rootbound.

ROOT PRUNING. Cutting the roots of a container plant done to help keep the plant small, make room in the container for fresh soil, and promote the growth of new feeder roots.

ROOTSTOCK. The lower part of a tree that supplies the roots onto which the desired fruiting variety is grafted. The rootstock imparts desirable traits to the grafted tree, such as small size, winter hardiness, early fruit production, or tolerance for heavy soils.

RUSSETING. A brownish roughened area on the skin of fruit that is characteristic to some varieties of fruit or can be caused by injury of some kind.

SCAFFOLD. A main structural branch.

SELF-FERTILE (OR SELF-FRUITFUL). A fruit tree that is able to produce fruit with pollen from its own flowers.

SEMI-DWARF. A tree that usually grows to between 40 percent and 75 percent of the size of a standard-sized tree because it has been grafted onto a dwarf rootstock.

SHOOT. A young stem or branch with its leaves. "Shoot" often refers to the amount of new growth in one season (the current season's growth) or in winter the growth made the previous season.

SOAKER HOSE. A low-volume irrigation hose laid on top of the ground that lets water seep out from many small holes along its length.

SOIL AMENDMENT. Anything added to soil to change or improve its physical or chemical properties.

SPECIES. A category of biological classification ranking below the genus or subgenus, consisting of related organisms capable of interbreeding. An apple is identified by genus and species names *Malus domestica*. The genus and species could be followed by the variety (*Malus domestica* Cox's Pippin).

SPORE. The reproductive body of a fungi or bacteria or certain other organisms.

SPUR. The short, stubby branches that produce clusters of buds, flowers, and fruit.

STANDARD. The size a tree will grow to if it is not grafted onto a dwarf rootstock. A standard-sized tree usually originates from a seed and produces roots that cause high vigor and size.

STONE FRUIT. Any fruit with a hard pit that surrounds the seed, such as peach, plum, and cherry.

SUCKER. A vigorous shoot growing from the base of the tree or from below the soil near the base of the tree.

SUMMER PRUNING. Pruning done from early spring and through summer to help keep trees small, to let light and air into the tree, and to train young trees.

TEMPERATE ZONE. The region between the Tropic of Cancer and the Arctic Circle in the Northern Hemisphere with a climate that is warm and mostly dry in the summers, cold and wet in the winters, and moderate in the spring and fall seasons.

TERMINAL BUD. The bud at the end of the branch. It develops new shoot growth when it grows.

THINNING. Removing excess immature fruit from the tree to increase fruit size, to minimize insect or disease damage, and to relieve excess weight on limbs. "Thinning" also refers to cutting out leaves and branches to let light into the tree's interior.

VARIETY. A taxonomic category of members of a species that differ from others of the same species in minor but heritable characteristics. In common usage, a "variety" is the same as a "cultivar."

VECTOR. In this case, referring to an organism such as an insect that transmits pollen from flower to flower.

VERMICULTURE. The cultivation of worms (usually red wigglers but not earthworms) to produce vermicompost (worm castings) or liquid fertilizer to use to nourish plants and trees.

VIGOROUS. When speaking of trees, a vigorous tree produces healthy and fast-growing vegetation.

WATERSPROUT. A rapidly growing and vigorous shoot growing from the trunk or branch of a tree.

WHIP. Usually a one-year-old tree with few or no branches and a trunk that is from a half-inch to three-quarters of an inch in diameter.

WHIP GRAFTING. A grafting method that uses a long, angled cut on a branch that was pruned from one tree and matched to a similar cut on the branch of a growing tree so that when the branches are joined and wrapped, the cambium layers will grow together to form one branch.

Resources

Nurseries

California

Berkeley Horticultural Nursery
1310 McGee Avenue
Berkeley, CA 94703
(510) 526-4704
www.berkeleyhort.com

Greenmantle Nursery
3010 Ettersburg Road
Garberville, CA 95542
(707) 986-7504
www.greenmantlenursery.com

Mid City Nursery, Inc.
3635 Broadway
American Canyon, CA 94589
(707) 642-4167
www.midcitynursery.com

Rolling River Nursery
(USDA certified organic nursery)
P.O. Box 332
Orleans, CA 95556
(530) 627-3120
www.rollingrivernursery.com

Urban Tree Farm Nursery
3010 Fulton Road
Fulton, CA 95439
(707) 544-4446
www.urbantreefarm.com

Oregon

One Green World
28696 S Cramer Road
Molalla, OR 97038
(877) 353-4028
www.onegreenworld.com

Washington

Burnt Ridge Nursery and Orchards
432 Burnt Ridge Road
Onalaska, WA 98570
(360) 985-2873
www.burntridgenursery.com

Raintree Nursery
391 Butts Road
Morton, WA 98356
(800) 391-8892
www.raintreenursery.com

British Columbia

One Shop in the Garden
6804 SW Marine Drive
Vancouver, BC V6R 1T2
(604) 822-4529
www.botanicalgarden.ubc.ca/
shop-in-the-garden

Restaurants

California

Bar Bambino
(Chef Lizzie Binder)
2931 16th Street
San Francisco, CA 94103
(415) 701-8466
www.barbambino.com

Flour +Water
(Chef Thomas McNaughton)
2401 Harrison Street
San Francisco, CA 94110
(415) 826-7000
www.flourandwater.com

Zuni Café
(Executive Chef Judy Rodgers)
1658 Market Street
San Francisco, CA 94102
(415) 552-2522
www.zunicafe.com

Oregon

Café Velo
(Chef Rick Wilson)
600 SW Pine Street
Portland, OR 97205
(503) 719-0287
www.cafe-velo.com

Grüner
(Chef Chris Israel)
527 SW 12th Avenue
Portland, OR 97205
(503) 241-7163
www.grunerpdx.com

Nostrana
(Executive Chef Cathy Whims)
1401 SE Morrison Street
Portland, OR 97214
(503) 234-2427
www.nostrana.com

Washington

Columbia City Bakery
(Pastry Chef Karra Wise)
4865 Rainier Avenue S
Seattle, WA 98118
(206) 723-6023
www.columbiacitybakery.com

Dahlia Lounge
(Executive Chef Tom Douglas)
2001 4th Ave
Seattle, WA 98121
(206) 682-4142
www.tomdouglas.com

The Mark Restaurant
(Executive Chef Lisa Scott Owens)
407 Columbia Street SW
Olympia, WA 98501
(360) 754-4414
www.themarkolympia.com

Poppy
(Chef Jerry Traunfeld)
622 Broadway E
Seattle, WA 98102
(206) 324-1108
www.poppyseattle.com

Staple & Fancy Mercantile
(Chef Ethan Stowell)
4739 Ballard Ave NW
Seattle, WA 98107
(206) 789-1200
www.ethanstowellrestaurants.com

Volunteer Park Café
(Pastry Chef Heather Earnhardt)
1501 17th Avenue E
Seattle, WA 98112
(206) 328-3155
www.alwaysfreshgoodness.com

The Walrus and the Carpenter
(Chef Renee Erickson)
4743 Ballard Avenue NW
Seattle, WA 98107
(206) 395-9227
www.thewalrusbar.com

British Columbia

Araxi Restaurant + Bar
(Executive Chef James Walt and Pastry Chef Aaron Heath)
4222 Village Square
Whistler, BC V0N 1B4
(604) 932-4540
www.araxi.com

Blue Water Cafe + Raw Bar
(Executive Chef Frank Pabst)
1095 Hamilton Street
Vancouver, BC V6B 5T4
(604) 688-8078
www.bluewatercafe.net

Thierry
(Pastry Chef Thierry Busset)
1059 Alberni Street
Vancouver, BC V6E 1A1
www.thierrychocolates.com

West Restaurant + Bar
(Pastry Chef Rhonda Viani)
2881 Granville Street
Vancouver, BC V6H 3J4
(604) 738-8938
www.westrestaurant.com

Books and Other Media

Appelhof, Mary.
Worms Eat My Garbage: How to Set Up and Maintain a Worm Composting System.
Kalamazoo, MI: Flower Press, 1982.

Douglas, Tom.
Tom's Big Dinners: Big-Time Home Cooking for Family and Friends. New York: Morrow, 2003.

Ellis, Barbara W., Fern Marshal Bradley, and Deborah L. Martin, eds. *The Organic Gardener's Handbook of Natural Insect and Disease Control.*
New York: Rodale Press, 2009.

Ingels, Chuck, P. Geisel, and M. Norton.
The Home Orchard: Growing Your Own Deciduous Fruit and Nut Trees.
Oakland: University of California Agriculture and Natural Resources, 2007.

Katzen, Mollie.
Still Life with Menu.
Berkeley, CA: Ten Speed Press,
1988.

Manning, Ivy.
Farm to Table Cookbook:
The Art of Eating Locally.
Seattle: Sasquatch Books, 2008.

Moulton, Gary.
Easy Steps to Fruit Tree
Pruning. DVD. (Available at
Raintree Nursery)

Otto, Stella.
The Backyard Orchardist:
A Complete Guide to Growing
Fruit Trees in the Home Garden.
Maple City, MI: OttoGraphics,
1993.

Pennington, Amy.
Urban Pantry: Tips and Recipes
for a Thrifty, Sustainable,
and Seasonal Kitchen.
Seattle: Skipstone, 2010.

Proulx, Annie, and Lew Nichols.
Cider: Making, Using, and
Enjoying Sweet and Hard Cider.
North Adams, MA : Storey
Publishing, 2003.

Richardson, Julie,
and Cory Schreiber.
Rustic Fruit Desserts:
Crumbles, Buckles, Cobblers,
Pandowdies, and More.
Berkeley, CA: Ten Speed Press,
2009.

Rodgers, Judy.
The Zuni Café Cookbook.
New York: W. W. Norton &
Company, 2002.

Stebbins, Robert L.,
and Lance Walheim.
Western Fruit, Berries and Nuts:
How to Select, Grow, and Enjoy.
Tucson, AZ: HP Trade, 1987.

Stowell, Ethan.
Ethan Stowell's New
Italian Kitchen.
Berkeley, CA: Ten Speed Press,
2010.

Other Resources

Ann Ralph
Fruit Tree Consultant
www.littlefruittree.com

California Rare Fruit
Growers, Inc.
The Fullerton Arboretum—CSUF
P.O. Box 6850
Fullerton, CA 92834
www.crfg.org

Center for Ecoliteracy
The David Brower Center
www.ecoliteracy.org

Elizabeth C. Miller Library
University of Washington
Botanical Gardens
3501 NE 41st St
Seattle, WA 98195
(206) 543-0415
depts.washington.edu/hortlib

Home Orchard Society
P.O. Box 230192
Tigard, OR 97281
www.homeorchardsociety.org

North American Fruit Explorers
www.nafex.org

Planet Natural
1251 N Rouse Ave
Bozeman, MT 59715
(800) 289-6656
www.planetnatural.com
(to order *Trichogramma* wasps)

University of British Columbia
Botanical Garden discussion
forums and hortline
www.ubcbotanicalgarden.org/
forums
www.botanicalgarden.ubc.ca./
hortline

Urban Agriculture Notes
www.cityfarmer.org/wormcomp61
(information about worm
composting from Canada's Office
of Urban Agriculture)

Western Washington Fruit
Research Foundation
29838 Marine View Drive SW
Federal Way, WA 98023
www.wwfrf.org
arbogast@fidalgo.net

Index

Credits

We are grateful to Schroder Music Company for allowing the use of a verse from "If You Love Me" at the beginning of this book: Words and music by Malvina Reynolds; copyright 1974 Schroder Music Co. (ASCAP). Renewed 2002; available on the CD, *Malvina Reynolds… Sings the Truth*, OMNI Records (2008). Used by permission. All rights reserved.

Thanks to Tom Douglas for his Persimmon Pudding with Pear Brandy Hard Sauce recipe from *Tom's Big Dinners: Big-Time Home Cooking for Family and Friends*, copyright © 2002 by Tom Douglas. Used by permission of the author.

And to Judy Rodgers for her Plum Sorbet recipe from *The Zuni Café Cookbook*, copyright © 2003 by Jody Rodgers. Used by permission of W.W. Norton & Company, Inc.

And to Cory Schreiber and Julie Richardson for their Nectarine, Boysenberry, and Almond Crisp recipe from *Rustic Fruit Desserts: Crumbles, Buckles, Cobblers, Pandowdies, and More*, copyright © 2009 by Cory Schreiber and Julie Richardson.

And to Mollie Katzen for her Golden Pear Soup recipe from *Still Life with Menu Cookbook*, copyright © 1988, 1994 by Tante Malka, Inc. Both used by permission of Ten Speed Press, an imprint of the Crown Publishing Group, a division of Random House, Inc.

Authors Barbara Edwards and Mary Olivella

BARBARA EDWARDS planted a Cox's Pippin apple tree when her first child was born and has been expanding her garden ever since. A public school teacher for many years, and an early participant in the Center for Ecoliteracy, she has long been an advocate of school gardens and sustainability projects. Barbara initiated a garden and nutrition project that incorporated school-grown organic food into the lunch program, helping spark a healthy eating trend in the Berkeley school district that is still going strong. She now teaches adults and tends a productive vegetable garden and an ever-increasing orchard of more than thirty fruit trees—all of them under ten feet tall—growing on her small urban lot.

MARY OLIVELLA grew up in Central America, where tropical gardens pretty much grow themselves. Upon moving to Northern California and meeting the challenges of growing edibles in this coastal climate, she became one of the early apprentices in the pioneering Garden Project at the University of California in Santa Cruz. The Garden Project was started by Alan Chadwick, a leading innovator in organic and sustainable farming techniques for the modern era. The fruit trees Mary planted there later inspired her to put down (tree) roots in her own garden in the San Francisco Bay Area. At the end of the day, when she transitions from working with MomsRising.org and other organizations that serve the public good, Mary can be found in her backyard. She continues to be in awe of the cycles of life at play among the plants.

LESLIE MILLER adores working on all food-related projects, including gathering recipes for *From Tree to Table*. The published author of many articles, essays, and books, she is the coauthor of *Ethan Stowell's New Italian Kitchen* and the editor of *Women Who Eat: A New Generation on the Glory of Food*. Miller is cofounder and partner in the editorial and writing company Girl Friday Productions in Seattle, where she defends her cherries from starlings as best she can.

Urban Pantry: Tips & Recipes for a Thrifty, Sustainable & Seasonal Kitchen
Amy Pennington
A modern, sustainable approach for stocking an efficient kitchen.

Eat Where You Live: How to Find and Enjoy Local and Sustainable Food No Matter Where You Live
Lou Bendrick
A user-friendly field guide for eating healthy, locally grown foods regardless of where you live.

Pacific Feast: A Cook's Guide to West Coast Foraging and Cuisine
Jennifer Hahn; Photography by Mac Smith
An inspiring yet informative guide to harvesting and cooking wild foods from beach to forest.

Edible Heirlooms: Heritage Vegetables for the Maritime Garden
Bill Thorness; Illustrations by Susie Thorness
The West Coast gardener's guide to growing heirloom plants.

Chefs on the Farm: Recipes and Inspiration from the Quillisascut Farm School of the Domestic Arts
Shannon Borg, Lora Lea Misterly, and Karen Jurgensen; Photographs by Harley Soltes
A visually rich tour of an organic farm, where award-winning chefs learn sustainable food practices.

Your Green Abode: A Practical Guide to a Sustainable Home
Tara Rae Miner
A down-to-earth guide to giving your home, condo, or apartment an eco-makeover.

SKIPSTONE

www.skipstonebooks.org
www.mountaineersbooks.org
800-553-4453